HIS
NEEDS,
HER
NEEDS

REVISED AND UPDATED

HIS NEEDS, HER NEEDS

Making Romantic Love Last

WILLARD F. HARLEY, JR.

Revell

a division of Baker Publishing Group
Grand Rapids, Michigan

© 1986, 1994, 2001, 2011, 2020, 2022 by Willard F. Harley, Jr.

Published by Revell
a division of Baker Publishing Group
PO Box 6287, Grand Rapids, MI 49516-6287
www.revellbooks.com

Printed in the United States of America

Library of Congress Cataloging-in-Publication Data
Names: Harley, Willard F., author.
Title: His needs, her needs : making romantic love last / Willard F. Harley, Jr.
Description: Revised and updated [edition]. | Grand Rapids, MI : Revell, a division of Baker
    Publishing Group, [2022]
Identifiers: LCCN 2021045640 | ISBN 9780800740993 (cloth) | ISBN 9781493434374 (ebook)
Subjects: LCSH: Marriage—United States. | Communication in marriage—United States. |
    Married people—United States—Psychology.
Classification: LCC HQ734 .H285 2022 | DDC 306.810973--dc23
LC record available at https://lccn.loc.gov/2021045640

ISBN 978-0-8007-4175-4 (ITPE)

The names and details of the people and situations described in this book have been changed or presented in composite form in order to ensure the privacy of those with whom the author has worked.

Baker Publishing Group publications use paper produced from sustainable forestry practices and post-consumer waste whenever possible.

22   23   24   25   26   27   28   7   6   5   4   3   2   1

Contents

Contents

Preface

In 1978, I was asked to teach a thirteen-week course on marriage at the church I attended. The topic was "What must a couple do to stay happily married?" The Christian education director tape-recorded the course for me.

Over the next few years, I used those tapes in my counseling practice to support the advice that I gave couples. One couple volunteered to transcribe the tapes so that I could give them to other couples in written form.

In 1984, that rough transcription made its way into the hands of an employee of the Fleming H. Revell Publishing Company, that person passed it on to the acquisitions editor, and the rest is history. It was published in 1986 with the title *His Needs, Her Needs: Building an Affair-Proof Marriage.*

Within two years of its first printing, the book became a bestseller, and it continues to be one of the most popular books on marriage right up to this year. It's been translated into twenty-two languages, and more than three million copies have been sold worldwide.

Finding a publisher for this book was the easy part—it almost fell into my lap. The hard part had been finding the answer to the question "What must a couple do to stay happily married?" which was the topic of the thirteen-week course I taught at my church.

Learning What Makes Marriages Succeed

When I was nineteen, a married acquaintance in college told me his marriage was in trouble and asked for my advice. The advice I gave did not help—his marriage ended in divorce. But my friend's marital failure started me thinking: What was wrong with the advice I gave? What makes some marriages succeed and others, like my friend's, fail?

It was 1960, and I was about to witness something that few expected—the beginning of the end of the traditional nuclear family in America. Evidence of this social disaster accumulated over the next twenty years. The divorce rate climbed from about 10 percent to over 50 percent, and the percentage of single adults increased from 6.5 percent to 20 percent. While the divorce rate finally stabilized at about 45 percent in 1980, the percentage of single adults has continued to increase right up to the present. It is currently at about 50 percent and climbing because fewer and fewer people are willing to commit themselves to one partner for life.

At the time, I didn't know that my friend's marital failure was part of a trend that was about to overwhelm nuclear families. I was unaware of new cultural forces that would threaten marriages as never before. Marriage counselors had it easy prior to that time because people simply didn't want to divorce, regardless of how unhappy they were. But now, they were unwilling to tolerate an unfulfilling marriage. So if a marriage was to be saved, a counselor had to know what made marriages fulfilling for both spouses. At the age of nineteen, I certainly did not have that answer.

Over the next few years, couples continued asking for my advice regarding marriage—especially after I earned a PhD in psychology. But I wasn't any more successful with them than I had been with my friend years earlier.

So I decided to become a marriage "expert." I read books written by the most prominent marital theorists and practitioners. I learned the latest techniques in helping spouses communicate with respect and understanding. I enrolled in a two-year internship at a clinic that had one of the best reputations for marital therapy and was supervised by the chairman of the University of Minnesota's Department of Family Social Science. But even after helping couples learn to communicate effectively, I was still unable to save their marriages. Almost everyone who came to me for help either ended up like my college friend—divorced—or simply continued to be in an unfulfilling marriage. I knew about my failure because I was doing something that very few other counselors did: I followed up on everyone I counseled long after they had made their last appointment.

I followed up not only with the couples I counseled but also with the couples of other counselors in the clinic where I interned. To my utter surprise, almost everyone else working with me in the clinic was failing as well! My supervisor was failing, the director of the clinic was failing, and so were the other marriage counselors who worked with me.

And then I made the most astonishing discovery of all. *Most of the marriage experts in America were also failing*. It was very difficult to find anyone willing to admit their failure, but when I had access to actual cases, I couldn't find any therapist who could prove that the counseling provided was any better than no counseling at all.

Many of these "experts" didn't even know how to make their own marriages work. The clinic director divorced while I was working there. Many others had been divorced themselves—several times.

Marital therapy had the lowest success rate of *any* form of therapy at that time. In one 1965 study I read, less than 25 percent of those surveyed felt that marriage counseling did them any good whatsoever, and a higher percentage felt that it did them more harm than good. It seemed that marriage counseling made couples *more likely* to divorce.

By 1975, I finally began to discover why I and so many other marital therapists were having trouble saving marriages: we did not understand what made a marriage work. We were all so preoccupied with what caused them to fail that we overlooked what helped them succeed. Many marriage counselors, myself included, thought that a lack of communication and problem-solving skills was causing these marriages to fail. So my goal had been to teach these couples how to communicate, to stop fighting, and to resolve conflicts.

But when I asked spouses why they had married in the first place, it wasn't because of great problem-solving skills. It was because they were in love. And over the years, they had somehow lost their love for each other. In fact, some had even come to hate each other.

When I asked spouses what it would take for them to be happily married again, most couldn't imagine that ever happening. But I persisted, and as the spouses reflected on it, they came to the realization that they would need to be in love again.

The poor communication that was apparent in many of these failed marriages had contributed to their loss of love, but it was also a symptom of their lost love. Spouses who fall out of love tend to fight instead of resolving their conflicts the right way—with care and respect. So if I wanted to save marriages, I would have to go beyond improving communication—I would have to learn how to restore love.

With this insight, I began to attack emotional issues rather than rational issues. My primary goal in marital therapy changed from resolving conflicts to restoring the feeling of love—romantic love. If I could help restore romantic love, I reasoned, then conflicts might not be as great an issue.

My background as a psychologist taught me that learned associations trigger most of our emotional reactions. Whenever something is presented repeatedly with a physically induced emotion, it tends to trigger that emotion all by itself. For example, if you are flashed the color blue along with an electric shock, and the color red along with a soothing back rub, eventually the color blue will tend to upset you and the color red will tend to relax you.

Applying the same principle to the feeling of love, I theorized that romantic love might be nothing more than a learned association. If someone were to do something or be something that made me feel good, then the person's presence in general might be enough to trigger a good feeling. But if that person were to make me feel especially good, then the association might make me feel especially good—something we have come to know as the feeling of love.

My theory could not have been more correct. If each spouse tried to do whatever it took to make the other happy and avoided doing what made the other unhappy, their feeling of love could be restored. The first couple I counseled with this new approach fell in love again, and their marriage was saved. From that point on, every time I saw a couple, I simply asked them what the other could do that would make them the happiest, and whatever it was, that was their first assignment.

Of course, not every couple really knew what would make them happy, and not every spouse was willing to try doing it. But as I perfected my method, I began to understand what it was that husbands and wives needed from each other to trigger the feeling of love. I helped them identify what each of them needed and also became more effective in motivating them to meet whatever need was identified, even when they didn't feel like doing it at first. Before long, my method helped almost every couple fall in love again and avoid divorce.

My method proved to be so successful that I stopped teaching psychology and started counseling full-time. As you can imagine, there were more couples wanting help from me than I could possibly counsel. It was then that I was asked to teach the thirteen-week course at my church: What must a couple do to stay happily married?

Thirty-Five Years and Counting

Some surveys have found this book to be the most effective book on marriage ever written. Couples report that by reading this book and following its guidance, their love has been restored and their marriages have been saved. That's because it gets right to the heart of what makes marriages work—the feeling of love and what couples must do to create and sustain that feeling.

Romantic love is a litmus test that reveals the right way for spouses to demonstrate their care for each other. If you're in love, you are caring for each other the right way. If you're not in love, your care for each other is missing the mark. This book will teach you how to care for each other in a way that will create and sustain romantic love and that will make your marriage fulfilling and secure.

Introduction

What is marriage? Its definition has been debated as never before by politicians, theologians, philosophers, judges, scientists, and therapists, just to name a few. There are many today who are not quite sure what it is. You might be among them. And yet, if I am to offer my help in creating a fulfilling marriage for you, we should begin by agreeing on what it is. Right?

So I come to you with a definition of marriage that I don't think you will question. It includes what almost everyone expects to give and receive when they marry.

Marriage is a relationship of mutual extraordinary care.

I've found that when the care that is expected by both spouses on their wedding day is given throughout their lives together, their marriage is fulfilling—and it lasts. But something else also lasts: their feeling of incredible attraction for each other—romantic love. In all the books I have written, I teach spouses how to provide mutual extraordinary care, and when they do, their marriage becomes everything they ever wanted or expected it to be.

There are three different expressions of that care: emotional care, protection, and partnership.

- *Emotional care* involves being each other's greatest source of happiness by meeting each other's most important emotional needs.

13

- *Protection* involves avoiding being each other's source of unhappiness by eliminating habits that I call Love Busters.
- *Partnership* involves making decisions that are coordinated and benefit both of you instead of only one of you.

While all three of these aspects of extraordinary care are *very important* in marriage, the first one is *crucial* in creating the feeling of love. That's the purpose of this book—to teach you how to provide the first expression of extraordinary care: emotional care. You and your spouse will discover and then learn to meet each other's most important emotional needs.

When you were first married, you assumed that those needs would be met, but for a variety of reasons, you may have become disappointed— perhaps disappointed enough to occasionally wonder why you were married in the first place. Ignorance usually contributes to this failure because men and women have great difficulty understanding and appreciating the importance of each other's emotional needs. Men tend to try to meet needs that they value, and women do the same. But the most important emotional needs of men and women are usually very different, and by trying to meet needs that matter less instead of those that matter more, spouses become very frustrated. The effort they put into caring for each other doesn't yield the appreciation they expect to see. Over time, many simply give up trying altogether when their effort doesn't seem to matter.

There are two reasons that a husband and a wife should meet each other's most important emotional needs. First, promises are made to meet certain emotional needs in an exclusive way. These promises are made to establish the nature of the relationship. It is secure and permanent, necessary ingredients for a lifelong marital relationship. But when those promises are not kept, spouses become confused and disillusioned. It's not fair. They've given each other the exclusive right to meet certain emotional needs without having ethical alternatives. Must they go through life without those needs met? When a commitment is made to be an exclusive provider of care, that care should be provided.

But there is a second reason that I will explain more clearly in the pages of this book: when you meet each other's most important emotional needs, you create and sustain a feeling of love for each other—romantic love—that is essential in a fulfilling marriage. I want you both to experience it through-out your life together.

Romantic Love Is Essential in Marriage

The feeling of being in love with someone is a remarkable experience. It's that very emotion that encourages two people to consider spending the rest of their lives together before they marry.

But in most marriages, spouses lose that feeling for each other within the first few years. That's because they don't understand what it was they did to trigger their feeling of love for each other while they were dating. After marriage, usually out of ignorance, they stop doing it for each other.

Should staying in love with each other matter? Consider this: I've never witnessed a single couple in love who divorced. Not one. It is the single most important factor in making a marriage secure.

But there are those who suggest that the loss of romantic love is not important and should be expected in marriage. When that happens, they encourage couples to move on to what they believe is a more mature, loveless marriage. These people are ignoring the facts: a loveless marriage usually ends in divorce or permanent separation.

Prior to marriage, the feeling of love is usually regarded as essential be-fore making that commitment. You may be asked by your family and friends, "Are you in love with the person you are about to marry?" If you are, then go for it. To them, it means that you're right for each other. If you are not in love, you are usually discouraged from going ahead with the marriage.

Are couples in premarital counseling warned that their feeling of love will eventually disappear? That they should prepare for a loveless mar-riage after a few years? No. If that were explained, it would be one of the quickest ways to encourage couples to call the wedding off. No one wants to look forward to a loveless marriage.

Instead, most premarital counseling leads couples to assume that their relationship will retain their feeling of romantic love. It's only after marriage that counselors introduce the idea that romantic love is not sustainable.

But my personal experience and the experience of about 20 percent of all married couples are proof to the contrary. Romantic love is sustainable.

Falling in love with each other mattered before you married. What matters even more, however, is *staying in love* with each other after you marry.

How to Fall in Love and Stay in Love

It was so easy for you and your spouse to fall in love with each other that you may have thought that staying in love would be just as easy—you were made to be together. It's the effortlessness of falling in love while dating that masks exactly what you were doing for each other that triggered that reaction. Most people who fall in love can't really explain it, so it's no wonder they don't know how to stay in love or how to restore that feeling after it's been lost.

I didn't know the answer either. I was in love, but I didn't really know what my wife, Joyce, was doing to keep it that way. It took quite a bit of study on my part before I was able to figure it out for myself.

The most important part of what it takes to be in love is to be each other's greatest source of happiness—to meet each other's most important emotional needs. It's the first part of extraordinary care that I mentioned. As you read the following chapters, you will achieve that objective by first identifying and then learning how to meet each other's most important emotional needs.

But there's another important objective: you must also know how to protect each other—from yourselves. In marriage, you and your spouse are in a position to do more to hurt each other than anyone else you know. You can become each other's greatest source of *unhappiness*. That's why I've written a second book, *Love Busters*. If you know how to make each other happy by meeting each other's most important emotional needs but fail to avoid making each other unhappy, your skill and effort will be wasted.

You might think that making each other happy and avoiding making each other unhappy cover all the bases when it comes to creating romantic love. But there is yet one more consideration: conflict resolution. Every couple faces conflicts throughout their marriage. Joyce and I have a conflict just about every hour we're together. The way you go about resolving those conflicts has everything to do with extraordinary care. If you care for each other, you should learn to resolve them the right way—in a way that makes both of you happy with the outcome. But if you resolve them the wrong way, where one of you wins while the other loses, resentment is almost always the result.

So I've written a third book to address this expression of extraordinary care—partnership: *He Wins, She Wins: Learning the Art of Marital Negotiation*. It was written to help couples resolve conflicts with mutual extraordinary care.

You've married someone who is wonderfully different from you. That difference can be a great advantage for both of you. It's as if you are standing back-to-back, looking in opposite directions. You see an ocean, while your spouse sees mountains. If you respect each other's perspective and try to learn from it, you will gain a much fuller understanding of the problems you face and how to solve them. But if you think that your perspective is right and your spouse's perspective is wrong, you will miss much of what life has to offer you, and many of your conflicts will go unresolved.

You express your extraordinary care for each other by showing profound respect for each other's opinions and perspectives. That mutual respect can help you make much wiser decisions because they reflect your mutual wisdom instead of the wisdom of only one of you.

But mutual respect does something else: it creates a partnership in which both of you become united in the decisions you make. Instead of making choices that benefit only one of you, you are motivated through mutual care to want each other to benefit. That leads to win-win outcomes.

I've also written two workbooks to guide you through the chapters of these three books: *Five Steps to Romantic Love: A Workbook for Readers of Love Busters and His Needs, Her Needs* and *He Wins, She Wins Workbook: Practicing the Art of Marital Negotiation*.

I encourage you and your spouse to read these books together, complete the questionnaires, and answer the questions at the end of each chapter. You might even use different-colored highlighters as you read so each of you can let the other know what is most important to you. Keep these books in a place where you can refer to them regularly because you should be reminded of the lessons they will teach you.

You might think that all of this is just too complicated and too much trouble to understand and apply. But I can tell you from personal experience and the experiences of the thousands of couples I've counseled that being in love makes doing all that I recommend almost effortless. Granted, restoring your love for each other may require some reading and careful application of what you have read, but after your feeling of love for each other returns, your marriage will be not only fulfilling but also very easy to maintain. A marriage of extraordinary care is what marriage was and is meant to be. It's what most couples expect to experience when they say, "I do."

ONE

Your Love Bank Never Closes

U nfortunately, most of us don't realize what we're getting into when we say, "I do." We think the dynamics of a good marriage depend on some mysterious blend of the "right" people. Or if a marriage turns out badly, we call the two people "wrong" for each other. While it's true that two inherently incompatible people *might* marry, it's unusual. More often than not, being right or wrong for someone depends not on some mysterious compatibility quotient but on how you affect each other. If what you and your spouse do for each other makes you both happy and it doesn't make you unhappy, your marriage will be very fulfilling. The possibility of divorce will never cross your minds.

Sounds simple, doesn't it? Too simple, you might be thinking. You might also be thinking that making each other consistently happy is impossible. And that avoiding what might hurt each other is also impossible.

Granted, there may be speed bumps on the road of marriage. On rare occasions, you might slip up. But this goal of making each other happy and avoiding what makes each other unhappy has been achieved by millions of couples, and their marriages are everything they hoped they would be. This does, however, require skill that you may not have at this time.

What, then, if you are willing but unskilled? Good news! You can do something about it. Training is possible at any time. For that reason, I believe marriages that have been torpedoed by emotional neglect need not sink. They can be towed into dry dock, repaired, and refitted. Once refitted, they will sail farther and faster than at any previous time.

But first, to help couples understand how important it is to make each other happy and avoid making each other unhappy, I created a concept that I call the Love Bank.

Everyone Has a Love Bank

Figuratively speaking, I believe each of us has a Love Bank. It contains many different accounts, one for each person we know. Each person makes either deposits or withdrawals whenever we interact with them. Pleasant interactions result in deposits. Unpleasant interactions result in withdrawals.

In my Love Bank system, every deposit or withdrawal is worth a certain number of love units. If I meet a friend (we'll call him Jim), and the encounter leaves me feeling comfortable, one or two love units will be deposited in his account in my Love Bank. If the interchange makes me feel good, Jim's deposit in his account may be five love units. Very good gets ten or fifteen. Twenty units or more go in his account when he makes me feel exceptionally good.

Suppose, however, that I find myself feeling uncomfortable when I am with someone; we'll call her Jane. One or two love units are withdrawn from her account. If she makes me feel bad, five units are withdrawn. Very bad warrants a ten-unit withdrawal. If I consider my encounter with Jane among the worst experiences of my life, it would cost her at least a twenty-unit withdrawal and maybe a loss of much more.

As life goes on, the accounts in my Love Bank fluctuate. Some of my acquaintances build sizable deposits. Others remain in the black but have small balances because they make almost as many withdrawals as they do deposits.

But a third group goes into the red with me. That means they cause me much more discomfort than comfort when we are together. I don't feel good when I think of them, and as a result, I try to avoid being with them. In short, their accounts in my Love Bank are overdrawn.

This concept of the Love Bank is simply designed to underscore the fact that we affect each other emotionally with almost every encounter.

The accumulation of positive and negative experiences determines our emotional reaction to those we know. You are not actively aware of any of this, of course. You don't say to yourself, *Wow, that was a three-unit deposit!* or *Ugh! Minus four units for him.* Nonetheless, the love units keep coming in or going out.

A Love Bank Love Story

Two Love Banks constantly operate in marriage: his and hers. Let's take a look at the story of John and Mary to see what can happen to a couple's accounts.

When John meets Mary, he immediately feels something special. She is intelligent, beautiful, charming, and full of life. John's Love Bank instantly credits her account with ten love units.

A day or two later, John calls Mary and asks her for a date. She accepts, and as John hangs up, ten more units go into Mary's account.

On the date, they have a fabulous time. John rates it as one of the best experiences of his life. Twenty more units added to Mary's account bring her balance to forty love units. A second date is almost as good, and she gets fifteen more love units, bringing the balance to fifty-five.

But the next time John calls Mary for a date, she has to turn him down. She says she feels truly sorry, but she has a commitment she set up many weeks ago. She quickly adds that she is free the next night, if John would be interested. John is indeed interested and arranges to pick her up for dinner about eight o'clock.

What happens to Mary's account in John's Love Bank as a result of this slightly negative encounter?

She definitely sounded sorry she couldn't go out with me tonight, John muses. *I can't expect her to be available just any time. Besides, she did suggest that we go out tomorrow night. I'm sure she really likes me.*

Regardless of how much John tries to assure himself, the experience still leaves him feeling slightly uncomfortable. Mary's account in John's Love Bank is debited five units.

Over the next few months, John and Mary date regularly and often. The good and fabulous experiences far outnumber the occasional negative ones, and Mary's balance soon stands at five hundred love units. Only Sarah, an old flame whom John broke up with over a year ago, had ever accumulated more units in John's Love Bank.

After six more months, Mary's balance rises to one thousand love units, an all-time high total for any woman in John's life, well in excess of Sarah's balance. At this point, John feels something he has never felt before. He is in love and tells Mary that she is the most attractive, intelligent, sensitive, charming, and delightful woman he has ever met.

Mary's balance in John's Love Bank has breached what I call the *romantic love threshold*. When someone's account is above a certain balance, the feeling of romantic love is triggered.

John associates Mary with many positive—even fabulous—emotional experiences and only a few negative ones. He looks forward to each date with Mary, and his mind dwells on her when they are apart.

He begins to wonder what he would do if he ever lost her. He can't imagine going through the rest of his life without her. *With Mary at my side, I wouldn't need anything or anyone else in order to be happy*, John tells himself. Vivid thoughts of marriage form in his mind.

Meanwhile, John's account in Mary's Love Bank has grown steadily but not at quite the same pace. When they met, she found him quite attractive, and their first dates were very good experiences for her. Because his account is clearly positive, 250 units, but has not yet breached the romantic love threshold, she likes him but is not in love with him.

While Mary's account in John's Love Bank continues to grow, surpassing twelve hundred units, his account in her Love Bank begins to falter. He begins to criticize the she way she does things which makes Love Bank withdrawals. He also starts to focus his attention on her in a way that makes her feel uncomfortable and frightened. More Love Bank withdrawals.

So Mary abruptly tells John she needs a little breathing room. She suggests that they suspend their dating for a month or so and wonders if they should date other people during that time.

John feels devastated. This encounter registers as one of the all-time painful experiences of his life. Twenty units quickly come out of Mary's hefty account. A few days later, John calls Mary and tries to convince her to change her mind, but she remains firm. John calls several more times over the next week. Mary stands fast, and before John decides to leave her alone for a month, debits accumulate in Mary's account that total over one hundred units.

John spends the next month feeling miserable. But he is still deeply in love with Mary, whose balance in his Love Bank still remains high, above one thousand units, in spite of the recent withdrawals. John tries to date another woman, Jill, but she does not stand a chance. Because he is so crazy about Mary, he finds dating Jill to be a negative experience. Through no fault of her own, his dates with her accumulate nothing but debits in her account.

At the end of a month, John calls Mary. Her balance has remained above one thousand units because, while he has missed her, there have been no additional negative experiences to cause any more withdrawals. John feels ecstatic when Mary tells him that she has also missed him and accepts his invitation to a date the very next evening. All she needed, she says, was time to think things through and see clearly how she felt.

The first date after the month-long separation is a memorable experience. Subsequent dates seem better than ever. At the end of the year, Mary's balance in John's Love Bank has risen to two thousand units. At the same time, John's account in Mary's Love Bank has also risen steadily until it, too, has breached the romantic love threshold and is now at an all-time high of eleven hundred units. Mary also thinks of wedding bells.

One night, after dinner at their favorite restaurant, John proposes marriage. He tells Mary he wants to live his life for her happiness and assures her that if she will marry him, he will do whatever he can to make her happy and will never do anything to hurt her. She accepts his proposal, and after a brief engagement, they become husband and wife.

Beyond the Honeymoon

The first year of their marriage is an extremely happy one. Without really thinking about it, John and Mary meet each other's emotional needs quite well. John remains as affectionate and attentive to her needs as he was when they dated. Mary responds passionately during lovemaking. They spend considerable time together and share their hopes and dreams in long conversations. Mary takes tennis lessons so that she can keep up with John in his favorite recreational pastime.

John earns an excellent income as a computer analyst, and Mary works as an office manager at a mortgage company. They are both happy with their working arrangements, at least for the present.

During their first year of married bliss, what happens to the balances in their Love Banks? They are still increasing, but not at the rate they did before marriage. Their dates before marriage were especially designed to make each other feel terrific, but now they become focused on other priorities: careers, the possibility of children, housing, friends and relatives, and an assortment of other distractions that take their attention off each other when they spend time together. It's not uncommon for them to field text messages from others when they actually do have a date.

In spite of her reduced rate of deposits in John's Love Bank, Mary's balance still increases. At the end of their first year of marriage, her net gain from the previous year adds up to an additional one hundred units. That brings her overall balance to twenty-one hundred units. Approximately the same pattern holds true for John's account which rises to twelve hundred units. During the next four years, accounts in both Love Banks continue to rise, but ever so slowly.

On their fifth anniversary, John still feels madly in love with Mary, and she feels the same about him. They decide to start a family, and little Tiffany arrives as they start their sixth year of marriage.

Critical changes start taking place in that sixth year. Mary is still the joy of John's life, but he notices an increase in his "down times." While John loves Tiffany dearly, she still creates new demands for both John and Mary and takes away from the amount of attention they once had just for each other.

As a net result of all these common changes, Mary's balance in John's Love Bank drops by one hundred units over the year. The loss is not that significant—yet. Mary's balance still remains very high at two thousand units, and John feels deeply in love with her.

But around the time of Tiffany's second birthday, Mary gets restless. She wants to advance her career. She approaches John to see if he would support the idea of her going back to college, finishing her bachelor's degree, and possibly going on for a master's degree in business administration.

"It will take six years of classes," Mary explains. "But I'll quit my part-time job so I can concentrate on the baby during the day and take most of the classes at night."

John agrees to her idea enthusiastically. He enjoys a solid and stable income, and they can manage without Mary's paycheck. He will take care of Tiffany while Mary is at school and when she needs time on occasion to finish homework assignments.

No Time for Romance

Mary enrolls in classes and soon earns excellent grades. But those grades require sacrifice of attention and time. What bothers John the most is that Mary rarely seems to be in the mood to make love. John understands her dilemma. School consumes a lot of energy, and what is left she devotes to housekeeping and caring for Tiffany. By bedtime, Mary feels exhausted, and John doesn't want her to feel pressured to make love.

John makes the best of it with less frequent and more hurried lovemaking when he finds Mary in the mood, but he also misses the attention she used to give him and the tennis games they usually played on Saturday mornings. Now Mary seldom spends time with him and rarely plays tennis on Saturdays. Instead, on the weekends, she does housework and catches up on homework for her Monday classes.

John and Mary continue in this pattern for the next two years. Mary's account in John's Love Bank drops slowly but steadily. John begins wondering what happened to the woman he married. She seems lost in her books and doesn't want to discuss what she is learning with him.

"It's all stuff you had years ago," Mary tells him. "Besides, you're a math expert, and I'm not taking that much math."

Note that John's account in Mary's Love Bank holds steady because John is helping her meet a very special need in her life right now—completing her education. Mary realizes they haven't spent much time together, but she deeply appreciates all John's sacrifices and his apparent total commitment to his family.

Things will be better as soon as I get my degree, she tells herself. So Mary plunges into academia, not quite realizing how her husband feels.

But she does notice a change in the attention he gives her when they are together. He is less affectionate and certainly less conversant. He hardly ever sits down with her just to talk. The only time he seems to show much of an interest in her is when he wants to make love. Because it feels rushed and focused on him, she feels used rather than loved.

They have entered a marital negative feedback loop. The less Mary meets John's emotional needs because of her study schedule, the more her account in his Love Bank drops. The lower her account goes, the less motivated he is to meet her emotional needs, which causes a drop in his account in her Love Bank.

Eventually, their sizable Love Bank balances drop so low that they are no longer in love with each other. Can the love they once had be restored?

TWO

Romantic Relationships 101

I've never witnessed a single married couple in love get divorced.

That's why I can't emphasize enough the importance of being in love while married. It's what motivated you and your spouse to marry, and it's what will keep you married.

So my strategy for saving marriages has been to simply restore spouses' feelings of love for each other. When that happens, their risk of divorce comes to an end. It's been a very successful strategy throughout my entire career, in which I have helped save thousands of marriages.

But romantic love is only half the story when it comes to marriage. Remember how I defined marriage in the introduction? *Marriage is a relationship of extraordinary care.* Care is the other half of the story. In marriage, romantic love and caring love are both essential because they both depend on each other.

Caring love is a *decision* to protect, provide, and be there for someone to make their life more fulfilling. We care for our children in this way. We also care for those who are friends and even for those we don't know who need our help when we support charitable organizations.

Romantic love, on the other hand, is not a decision. It's a *feeling*. It's an emotional reaction to someone who has made enough Love Bank deposits in their account to breach the romantic love threshold. It's the feeling of incredible attraction to someone.

When two people marry, they make a decision to care for each other in an extraordinary way. It's what they expect to give and receive from each other. Without that promise and expectation, marriage would mean very little.

Caring love is such an important commitment that I define marriage as a relationship of extraordinary care, and few would disagree with me at the time of the wedding. Their commitment is to protect, provide, and be there for each other in an extraordinary way. They agree to provide a level of care for each other that is greater than their level of care for anyone else.

But while spouses can decide to provide caring love for each other, they cannot decide to have romantic love for each other. It's only when each spouse is able to make enough deposits to breach the romantic love threshold that they are able to trigger and maintain the feeling of romantic love.

Who is responsible for your feeling of romantic love? It's your *spouse*, not you. If you are in love with your spouse, they should get all the credit.

Who is responsible for your spouse's feeling of romantic love for you? It's *you*, not your spouse.

But what if you really do care for your spouse, and yet your spouse is not in love with you? Care comes in many forms, and there are many ways that we care for those we love. If your spouse is not in love with you, and you really do care for them, it's how you express your care that needs attention.

I'm assuming that you have already committed yourself to care for your spouse. Without that commitment, there is no book that can help your marriage. So I have written this book to help you understand and then apply how to care for your spouse in a way that will create the feeling of romantic love. To do that, let me explain what romantic relationships are.

My Early Interest in Romantic Relationships

My romantic relationship with my wife, Joyce, raised questions for me. How did I come to be so crazy about someone? Does she feel the same way? How long will it last?

Whenever Joyce broke up with me while we were dating (it happened on several occasions), I was devastated. Why did I feel that way, and what kept me coming back to her whenever she wanted to start our relationship up again?

These and many other questions inspired me to begin studying couples in a romantic relationship when I was a graduate school teaching assistant. I was fascinated by friends and students who seemed obsessed with romance. My interest continued as I taught psychology over the next ten years and conducted a series of formal studies with students who were in romantic relationships. When I operated mental health clinics in Minnesota, those studies continued. To this day, I find romantic relationships absolutely fascinating and am still learning about them.

Part of the reason for my continuing interest in romantic relationships is that I've found a romantic relationship to be the driving force for infidelity—the most painful and inexcusable betrayal in marriage. Shortly after I married Joyce, I became acutely aware of infidelity's destructive outcome when someone closely connected to us had an affair with a coworker. The strength of this romantic relationship tore everyone's life apart, and yet it could not be stopped. The affair seemed to be totally out of control. It was then that I came to understand the powerful force of a romantic relationship.

But the most important reason for my interest in romantic relationships is that, as a psychologist, I'm impressed by what a romantic relationship does for a marriage. It makes a marriage absolutely sensational. And as long as it lasts, the marriage lasts.

Let me begin by giving you my definition of a romantic relationship.

**A romantic relationship is between
two people in love who
meet each other's intimate emotional needs.**

I'll break down this definition into its primary parts: *romantic love* and *emotional needs*.

What Is "Being in Love"?

Let me begin with a definition of romantic love.

**Romantic love is the feeling of incredible attraction
to someone, usually of the opposite sex.**

In the early years of my study of romantic love, I developed a test to measure it. I called it the Love Bank Inventory. These are some of the questions in the inventory that those in love tend to answer with a truthful "definitely yes":

Do you usually have a good feeling whenever you think about _____?

Would you rather be with _____ than anyone else?

Do you enjoy telling _____ your deepest feelings and most private experiences?

Do you feel "chemistry" between you and _____?

Does _____ bring out the best in you?

I have used the Love Bank inventory to determine if spouses I'm counseling are making progress. As their scores increase, I know they're on the right track. When their scores reach a certain point, I know they have fallen in love, and they know it too.

If you are in love, you don't need a questionnaire to prove it. Romantic love is unmistakable for those who experience it. There is no doubt in their minds. So if someone isn't sure if they are in love, they are probably not in love.

Because I have learned how to measure romantic love for the couples I counsel, I've found that it can be created; it can be destroyed; it can be re-created; and it can be sustained indefinitely. It's all about Love Bank balances and keeping them above the romantic love threshold.

What Are Emotional Needs?

Let me offer a definition of an emotional need.

> An emotional need is a craving that, when satisfied,
> leaves us feeling happy and content;
> when it's unsatisfied, we feel unhappy and frustrated.

There are thousands of emotional needs: peanut butter sandwiches, birthday parties, football on TV. Any craving that makes you content when satisfied and frustrated when unsatisfied is an emotional need.

What cravings do spouses have in marriage? To answer that question, I asked hundreds of married couples what their spouse could do for them that would make them the happiest and most content. I also asked them what would make them the unhappiest and most frustrated when their spouse didn't do it. It was an open-ended question that allowed spouses to respond with many illustrations of what their spouse had done, or could do, that meant the most to them.

After accumulating thousands of examples, I asked a few of my student assistants to place them into categories. They discovered that almost all the examples fit into ten categories: admiration and appreciation, affection, intimate conversation, domestic support, family commitment, financial support, honesty and openness, physical attractiveness, recreational companionship, and sexual fulfillment. I called these categories the *important emotional needs* in marriage.

Using this list, I then asked spouses to rank them based on how much happiness and contentment they experienced when their spouse fulfilled each need and how much unhappiness and frustration they experienced when each need was not fulfilled. They ranked them from 1 to 10, with 1 being the most pleasure and 10 being the least pleasure.

All the categories represented emotional needs that, when met, provided enjoyment to almost all the spouses I surveyed. Very rarely did I find someone who indicated no need at all for one or more of the categories on the list. In other words, these categories represent universally accepted emotional needs that can be met in marriage.

But to my surprise, and to the surprise of my students, husbands and wives tended to rank the needs very differently. On average, wives ranked affection, intimate conversation, honesty and openness, financial support, and family commitment as their top five emotional needs. Husbands, on the other hand, tended to rank sexual fulfillment, recreational companionship, physical attractiveness, domestic support, and admiration and appreciation as their top five emotional needs.

What an insight! No wonder husbands and wives have so much difficulty meeting each other's needs. They are highly motivated to do for their spouse what they appreciate the most but much less motivated to do what their spouse appreciates most. They lack empathy.

With these results, I constructed the Emotional Needs Questionnaire, which you will find in appendix B, to identify the most important emotional needs for a particular couple. That way, each person could identify what their spouse could do for them that would make them the happiest and make the most Love Bank deposits.

I never tell couples what their most important emotional needs are or should be—they tell me whenever they complete the questionnaire. I have kept track of the way husbands and wives answer these questions for many years, and I am still finding that husbands tend to rank one set of five the highest, while wives tend to rank the other set the highest.

Pay careful attention to the next point I'm going to make, because it's one of the most misunderstood aspects of my program: *every person is unique*. While men on average pick five particular emotional needs as their most important and women on average pick another five, any individual can pick any combination of the basic ten. Although I have identified the most important emotional needs of the average man and woman, I don't know the emotional needs of any particular husband or wife. It's very important for each couple to complete their own questionnaires to gain insight into what they can do to make each other the happiest.

So whenever I refer to a particular need in this book as *his need* or *her need*, I'm not telling you what your emotional needs are or should be. You and your spouse should identify them for yourselves and then communicate them to each other. But I am warning you that, on average, husbands and wives have trouble meeting each other's emotional needs because they don't understand how important those needs are to each other.

What Are Intimate Emotional Needs?

I had identified the ten emotional needs that, when met in marriage, make the largest Love Bank deposits. But among those ten, four needs tended to be identified as making the very largest deposits for most couples, much more than any of the other six. For husbands, they tended to be the emotional needs for sexual fulfillment and recreational companionship, and for wives, they tended to be affection and intimate conversation. When those four emotional needs were met, they tended to make spouses the happiest and most fulfilled.

The more I studied romantic relationships, the more aware I became that those four emotional needs were almost always being met by couples in love. That made sense to me because they tended to make the largest Love Bank deposits for a man and a woman. With those large deposits, the romantic love threshold would be easily breached, and romantic love would be triggered and sustained.

When a husband and a wife meet each other's emotional needs, they are showing their caring love for each other. But since all emotional needs, when met, do not make the same Love Bank deposits, caring love must be very specific if a married couple wants to create and sustain romantic love. Spouses must care for each other in ways that make the largest Love Bank deposits so that their accounts stay above the romantic love threshold. While all ten emotional needs make some Love Bank deposits, the needs that make the most deposits, when met, tend to be affection, intimate conversation, sexual fulfillment, and recreational companionship—two needs for her and two needs for him.

I call these four emotional needs the *intimate emotional needs* because they appear to be essential ingredients in almost all romantic relationships. Without a doubt, a romantic relationship is intimate.

I made another observation in my study of romantic relationships: *the intimate emotional needs are much easier to meet when people are in love.*

Even though sexual fulfillment and recreational companionship are statistically less important to women than they are to men, women in love tend to fulfill those needs almost effortlessly. Similarly, the needs of affection and intimate conversation are met almost effortlessly by a man in love. It's as if their instincts to meet these needs kick in as soon as they are in love.

I came to realize that a romantic relationship is driven by an assortment of human instincts that encourage a couple to be together. The two people not only find each other irresistible but also are highly motivated to do what it takes to keep each other irresistible.

But spouses can fall out of love if they no longer have the opportunity to continue meeting each other's intimate emotional needs. It's as if the Love Bank has a monthly finance charge. If a couple is separated due to a career, as was the case with John and Mary, or if they find that other priorities in life are more important than spending time with each other, their Love Bank balances slowly drop until they fall below the romantic love threshold. When that happens, the instincts that make it easy to meet intimate emotional needs become dormant, and the needs become more difficult to meet for each other.

At that point, a man and a woman are tempted to take shortcuts. *I'd like you to meet my needs, but I don't have the time or energy to meet yours.* They begin to think that the other person's intimate emotional needs are not as important as they were in the past.

At night before going to sleep, a husband may have plenty of energy to make love but not enough to have an intimate conversation with his wife. A wife may find herself willing to talk with her husband but not willing to make love.

This common problem in marriage can be overcome by restoring romantic love. To achieve that objective, each spouse must put more effort into meeting the intimate emotional needs of the other spouse until the romantic love threshold is breached. Then it becomes much easier to meet those needs.

But that's easier said than done. Couples usually don't understand how the Love Bank works, and so they attribute their loss of love to having grown apart. They feel that if love is not natural (instinctive), it's not meant to be. *I've married the wrong person.*

In the next four chapters, we will look at the four intimate emotional needs grouped by the gender typically in greatest need of them: affection and intimate conversation for her, and sexual fulfillment and recreational companionship for him. Her needs will be presented together because they have so much in common, and I will present his needs together for the same reason.

If you and your spouse are not in love with each other, the following chapters will show you how to meet those intimate emotional needs for each other so that you can breach the romantic love threshold. If you are already in love, I will encourage you to continue meeting those needs regardless of obstacles so that you can maintain a romantic relationship for the rest of your lives.

The Policy of Undivided Attention

Before you and your spouse were married, you spent most of your recreational time together. You talked to each other almost every day about your deepest feelings. You were affectionate with each other whenever you were together. Sex was definitely on your minds. You scheduled time to give each other special attention.

But now that you are married, you may spend your most enjoyable recreational time apart. Your conversations may tend to be superficial and not very intimate. Your affection may have slipped. And sex? It's just not the same. You simply cannot find the time for recreation, affection, intimate conversation, or sexual fulfillment. They're no longer on your schedule.

Unless you and your spouse actually plan time to be together each week, as you did while dating, to meet each other's intimate emotional needs for affection, intimate conversation, sexual fulfillment, and recreational companionship, you will not meet them adequately for each other. And if you don't meet those needs for each other, staying in love will be a challenge.

To avoid that tragic outcome, I encourage couples to follow an essential rule for a fulfilling marriage. I call it the Policy of Undivided Attention.

> Give your spouse your undivided attention a minimum of fifteen hours each week, using the time to meet the intimate emotional needs of affection, intimate conversation, sexual fulfillment, and recreational companionship.

Your time together should be private if you are to meet each other's intimate emotional needs. You should not include children (who are awake), relatives, or friends.

The objective of your time together should be to meet all four of your intimate emotional needs: affection, intimate conversation, sexual fulfillment, and recreational companionship.

The total amount of time you spend together each week should reflect the quality of your marriage. If your marriage is satisfying to you and your spouse, fifteen hours will maintain your love for each other. But if you suffer from marital dissatisfaction, plan more time until marital satisfaction is achieved. Many couples find that being together for three to five hours at a time is the most fulfilling.

I call this time you spend together for undivided attention a romantic date. Both spouses find it to be romantic because each of them is having their most intimate emotional needs met.

If you want this time together to be a reality in your life, you must get it on your schedules immediately. And then perhaps every Sunday afternoon at 3:30, schedule at least fifteen hours of the coming week for your romantic dates. Document the time you spend together and hold each other accountable to make it happen.

I have written a series entitled *Dating the One You Married.* If you have difficulty finding the time to have a romantic date, or if you face other obstacles, I encourage you to read this series. It's available in the "Articles" section of the Marriage Builders website (www.marriagebuilders.com).

What about the Other Six Emotional Needs?

Love Bank deposits don't begin and end with the meeting of the four intimate emotional needs. There are many other ways that spouses make each other happy that are also important.

When I asked spouses what they could do to make each other happy, six other emotional needs were commonly expressed. These should not be ignored in marriage.

Three of the needs that tend to be more important to women than to men are honesty and openness, financial support, and family commitment. Men, on the other hand, often find physical attractiveness, domestic support, and admiration and appreciation to be more important. But, of course, all needs are specific to individual spouses and should be evaluated accordingly.

I advise spouses to put their greatest effort into meeting each other's top two emotional needs, which are usually the intimate emotional needs. Then they should learn to be very good at meeting each other's remaining emotional needs ranked 3 through 5. When those five emotional needs are met, romantic love is guaranteed.

This doesn't mean that the remaining five emotional needs are not at all important. It just means that your effort will not be appreciated as much and that not as many Love Bank deposits will be made. In so many marriages, spouses put too much effort into meeting needs that are rated low and not enough effort into meeting needs that are rated high. By understanding what your spouse needs the most from you and then learning how to meet those needs effectively, you won't make that mistake.

Chapters 3 through 6 explain how to meet the four intimate emotional needs. How to meet the remaining six emotional needs will be explained in the following chapters 7 through 12.

How Emotional Needs Are to Be Met: Quality, Quantity, and Mutuality

What does it take to become an expert at meeting your spouse's emotional needs? There are three basic goals you should consider: quality, quantity, and mutuality. You will be reminded of these goals as each of the ten emotional needs is discussed.

Quality means that you are meeting the emotional need effectively; your effort is hitting the mark; your spouse is fulfilled whenever you try to meet that need.

The chapters in this book will help you understand what it is that your spouse needs from you and how you can develop habits to meet those needs. Keep in mind that a new habit is formed by repetition. The more you do something, the stronger the habit becomes. I want you and your spouse to get into habits that make massive Love Bank deposits. Once you are in the habit of meeting each other's emotional needs, you will make deposits almost effortlessly.

Quantity refers to how often you or your spouse would like an emotional need met. For some emotional needs, like sexual fulfillment, once or twice a week is usually sufficient. For others, like affection, it might be several times a day.

The total time spent to meet an emotional need should also be understood. How long should your intimate conversation be? How much time should you plan for a recreational activity?

Mutuality is an extremely important goal as you learn to meet each other's emotional needs. It involves making the experience mutually enjoyable.

You won't get very far in learning a new habit if it's very unpleasant to do. You simply won't do it long enough for a habit to form. Granted, a new activity, like learning how to type, always seems a bit awkward. But it should get much easier and more enjoyable the more you practice it. If that's not the case, other ways of meeting the emotional need should be explored.

So as you are learning what you want from each other, you should have the right to refuse to do anything that is unpleasant. That doesn't mean the issue is no longer pursued. Instead, consider other alternatives that would be effective yet pleasant for you to do. Deposits should be made in both of your Love Banks when you meet each other's emotional needs.

THREE

Affection

When Jolene fell in love with Richard, she knew she had found the man she wanted to spend her life with. Ruggedly handsome, Richard was the strong, silent type, which made him even more intriguing to Jolene. Dates with Richard were exciting and passionate.

We've got the right chemistry, Jolene assured herself.

However, after just a few months of marriage, Jolene started noticing something a bit odd: whenever she cuddled up for a hug or a little kiss, Richard became sexually aroused almost immediately. Almost without exception, physical contact led straight to the bedroom.

Jolene also learned that Richard's "strong, silent" courting style had masked his tendencies for extreme moodiness and keeping almost everything to himself. Before they married, Richard had told Jolene that his mother had died when he was just ten and that his father and two older brothers had raised him. She hadn't thought too much of it at the time. But she eventually became aware of the effect it had on his ability to be affectionate with her.

Richard had grown up in a home where displays of affection were infrequent before his mother died and almost nonexistent afterward. He didn't know how to be affectionate because he had received so little himself. For him, affection in marriage was synonymous with sex, something that left Jolene feeling disillusioned, unfulfilled, and used. As Richard and Jolene approached their first anniversary, Richard's account in Jolene's Love Bank barely held its own.

Affection—the Cement of a Relationship

In the last chapter, I drew a distinction between romantic love and caring love. Romantic love is a *feeling* of incredible attraction, while caring love is a *decision* to protect, provide, and be there for someone to make their life more fulfilling. We care for our children in this way. Affection is the symbolic expression of caring love.

To most women, affection symbolizes security and protection—vitally important in their eyes. When a husband shows his wife affection, he sends the following messages:

- I care about you.
- You are important to me, and I don't want anything to happen to you.
- I'm concerned about the problems you face, and I'll try to help you overcome them.

A hug can say any and all of the above. Men need to understand how strongly women need these affirmations. For many women, there can hardly be enough of them.

I've mentioned hugging because I believe it is a skill most husbands need to develop to show their wives affection. It is also a simple but effective way to build the account in their wives' Love Banks.

Most women love to hug. They hug each other; they hug children, animals, relatives. But they can also become inhibited about hugging if they think it could be misinterpreted in a sexual way.

Obviously, a man can express affection in other ways that can be equally important to a woman. Flowers, a small gift, or a note expressing love and care can simply but effectively communicate the same message.

A sensitive husband may open the door for his wife as a way to tell her, "I love you and care about you."

Holding hands is a time-honored and effective sign of affection. Walks after dinner, back rubs, text messages, and conversations with thoughtful and loving expressions all add love units to the Love Bank. As more than one song has said, "There are a thousand ways to say I love you."

From a woman's point of view, affection is the essential cement of her relationship with a man. Without it, a woman usually feels alienated from her mate. With it, she becomes tightly bonded to him while he adds units to his Love Bank account.

But She Knows I'm Not the Affectionate Type

Most women find affection important in its own right. They love the feeling that accompanies both the giving and receiving of affection. Men should understand that it usually has nothing to do with sex. It's the same emotion women exchange with their children or pets.

All of this is often confusing to the husband. He may view affection as part of sexual foreplay, which can arouse him in a flash. He mistakenly assumes that affection serves the same purpose as initiating sex for women and has the same rapid arousal effect. So the only time these men are affectionate is when they want to make love.

But that kind of affection does not communicate, "I care about you." Instead, it communicates, "I want sex." Instead of giving, it's taking. That self-focused message is not lost on women who crave affection. A wife deeply resents her husband's use of such an important symbol of care only when he has a need for sex.

It gets much worse. While some men try to be affectionate only when they want sex, other men don't ever want to be affectionate. They don't think it should be necessary, even while having sex.

Let's look in on a hypothetical couple we'll call Brianna and Bruce. They have been having tension lately because Brianna hasn't responded with much enthusiasm to Bruce's requests for sex. As our scene opens, she senses Bruce has that look in his eye again, and she tries to head him off at the pass: "Bruce, let's just relax for a few minutes. I'm not ready for sex just like that. I need a little affection first."

Bruce bristles impatiently and says, "You've known me for years. I'm not the affectionate type, and I'm not going to start now!"

Does this sound incredible or far-fetched? I hear versions of this regularly in my office. Bruce fails to see the irony in wanting sex but refusing to give his wife affection. A man who growls, "I'm not the affectionate type" while reaching for his wife's body to satisfy his desires for sex is like a salesman who tries to close a deal by saying, "I'm not the friendly type—sign here, I've got another appointment waiting."

Any Man Can Learn to Be Affectionate

Affection is usually so important for women that they become confused when their husbands don't respond in kind. For example, a wife may call or text her husband while he's at work just to see if he's okay. She would love to receive the same from him. But perhaps he never calls from work to see how she's doing. Doesn't he care about her? Her husband may care deeply for her, but he doesn't express that care because his need for affection has a much lower priority.

When I go on a trip, I often find little notes Joyce has packed among my clothes. She is telling me she loves me, of course, but the notes send another message as well. Joyce would like to get the same notes from me, and I have tried to leave such notes behind—on her pillow, for example—when I go out of town.

My need for affection is not the same as hers, nor is it met in similar ways. I've had to discover these differences and act accordingly. For example, when we walk through a shopping center, it is important to her that I walk next to her and hold her hand. It's something that would not occur to me naturally or automatically. She has encouraged me to take her hand, and I'm glad to do so because I know she enjoys that and I enjoy it too. It says something I want to say and she wants to hear.

When I try to explain this kind of hand-holding to some husbands in my counseling office, they question my manhood a bit. Isn't my wife "leading me by the nose," so to speak? I reply that in my opinion nothing could be further from the truth. If holding Joyce's hand in a shopping center makes her feel loved and cherished, I would be a fool to refuse to do it. I appreciate her coaching on how to show affection. I promised to care for her when I married her, and I meant every word of it. If she explains how

I can best give her the care she wants, I'm willing to learn because I want her to be happy.

Almost all men need some instruction in how to become more affectionate, and those who have developed such loving habits have usually learned them from good coaches—perhaps former girlfriends. In most marriages, a man's wife can become his best teacher if he approaches her for help in the right way.

First, he needs to explain to her that he cares for her very much but often fails to express that deep care appropriately. Then he should ask her to help him learn to express this affection, which he already feels, in ways she will appreciate.

Initially, she will probably be puzzled by such a request. "When you love someone, affection comes naturally!" she may reply. She may not realize that affection comes more naturally for her than it does for him.

"I don't think I let you know how much I really care for you," he may answer. "I just assume you know because I help work for our family, take you out, and do my share around the house. I should be doing more to tell you how much I care about you."

"Sounds great! When do we start?"

She can help by making a list of the signs of care that mean the most to her. Women may express a need for physical closeness, such as hugging, hand-holding, and sitting close together. Kissing is very important to most women, as are token gifts and cards that express a husband's emotional attachment and commitment.

When Ted and Paula came to my office for help to improve affection, I gave Paula a form to complete, the Affection Inventory (you can find the form in *Five Steps to Romantic Love*), to help her identify acts of affection that were most important to her. The form consists of two parts: "Affectionate Habits to Create" and "Affectionate Habits to Avoid." Under "Affectionate Habits to Create," she wrote the following:

- Hug and kiss me every morning while we're still in bed.
- Talk with me and tell me that you care about me while we're having breakfast together.
- Hug and kiss me before you leave for work.

- Call or text me during the day to see how I'm doing and to tell me you care about me.
- After work, call or text me before you leave for home so that I can know when to expect you.
- When you arrive home from work, hug and kiss me and spend a few minutes talking to me about how my day went (I'll talk to you about how your day went too).
- Help me with the dishes after dinner.
- Hug and kiss me for at least five minutes when we go to bed at night and tell me that you care about me.
- Bring me flowers once in a while as a surprise (be sure to include a card that expresses your care for me).
- Remember my birthday, our anniversary, Christmas, Mother's Day, and Valentine's Day. Give me a card and a gift that is sentimental, not practical. Learn how to shop for me.

Under the heading "Affectionate Habits to Avoid," she wrote:

- Don't just tell me how attracted you are to my body when you want to express your affection.
- Don't touch my butt, breasts, or crotch when you are being affectionate with me (especially when we are washing the dishes together).

Ted could understand what Paula meant by her list of "Affectionate Habits to Create." And he was willing to try to learn to be more affectionate by practicing those behaviors until they became habits. But he was confused and somewhat offended by her entries under "Affectionate Habits to Avoid."

"Don't you want me to tell you how sexy you look to me? You turn me on, and I'm just following my instincts," he admitted.

"I want to be attractive to you," she replied. "But when we're together, you seem to be interested in *only* my body. It makes me feel like you don't care about me as a person."

I explained to Ted the difference between affection and admiration and appreciation (we will cover that need in chapter 12). Affection is the communication of care, while admiration and appreciation are the communication of respect and value. There was nothing wrong with Ted communicating his appreciation of the way Paula looked, but it didn't communicate his care for her.

Paula was starved for affection, which was her most important emotional need. Admiration and appreciation, on the other hand, were far down her list of needs that she wanted Ted to meet. Granted, some women with a high-priority need for admiration and appreciation want to be told regularly by their husbands how attractive they are. And some don't even mind being fondled while washing the dishes as evidence of that appreciation. But Ted's failure to provide affection along with Paula's very low need for admiration and appreciation made her feel particularly uncared for when he focused most of his attention on her physical attributes.

Is Affection Mutually Enjoyable?

The plan Paula gave Ted to meet her emotional need for affection defined two of the conditions that should be met—quality and quantity. She told him what she wanted him to do (quality) and how often she wanted him to do it (quantity). But what about the third condition, mutuality? How did Ted feel about being affectionate the way she wanted it and as often as she wanted it? If he was to develop the habit of being affectionate, he had to enjoy doing it.

I explained to Ted that a new behavior usually feels awkward at first. It doesn't feel right. But that doesn't mean he won't eventually enjoy doing it for her, unless something she is asking him to do is consistently unpleasant. In that case, they should work together to modify what she needs from him so that he can enjoy doing it for her.

Paula was also concerned about his attitude. If he didn't feel like being affectionate, how would following her advice meet her emotional need? It seemed too contrived.

But I explained to her that once they became habits for him, his affectionate behaviors would become more creative and personal. His sincerity would be clearly expressed in the way he was affectionate.

Ted really did care for Paula. She was important to him, and he was concerned about the problems she faced. He wanted to help her overcome them. But he had not learned how to express his care for her with acts of affection.

After helping Ted understand what Paula considered to be affection and not affection, I gave him a plan to turn those affectionate behaviors into habits. I used another form called Strategy to Meet the Need of Affection (you can find the form in *Five Steps to Romantic Love*). The strategy required him to keep the list of the affectionate behaviors she craved with him at all times. Every day the list reminded him of what she wanted him to do for her. From the moment he woke up in the morning by hugging and kissing her to the five-minute hug before they went to sleep at night, he was meeting her need for affection.

Eventually, the list was unnecessary. Ted successfully developed the habit of being an affectionate husband. He expressed his care for Paula almost effortlessly throughout every day, as it was a mutually enjoyable experience.

When Affection Is His Emotional Need

Occasionally, I counsel a couple and find that affection is one of the husband's most important emotional needs. He is not wanting affection as a prelude to sex but rather as a symbol of his wife's care for him. If his wife has a similar need for affection, it's not usually on their list of problems to solve. They already express their mutual affection toward each other.

But when the wife of this husband does not crave affection as much as he does, the solution is similar to the one used when the wife has a greater need for affection. In those more unusual cases, I encourage the wife to learn how to become an affectionate wife. She learns how to develop habits of affection that communicate her care for her husband.

Sex Begins with Affection

Affection is the *environment* of a marriage, while sex is an *event*. Affection is a way of life, a canopy that covers and protects a marriage. It's a direct and convincing expression of caring love that gives the event of sex a more appropriate context for most women.

Because men tend to translate affection into sex so readily, I put an emphasis on learning nonsexual affection. I try to teach a husband to make affection a way of expressing his care to his spouse. He learns not to just turn it on and off to get some sex. Whenever he and his spouse come together, a big hug and kiss should be routine. In fact, almost every interaction between them should include affectionate words and gestures. I believe every marriage should have an atmosphere that says, "I really care about you, and I know you care about me."

When I talk about nonsexual affection, many men become confused. What is he supposed to do with his natural feeling of sexual arousal, which can be triggered by almost any act of affection? He wants to know if he has to take cold showers to keep cool. I point out to him that when he was dating, he was just as sexually aroused as he is now, even more so! But he showed plenty of affection and attention that did not include groping and grabbing. He treated the woman he loved with respect and tenderness.

Many husbands remember the passionate encounters of their courting days and want to know, "Why doesn't she get turned on the way she did before we were married?"

I give them the answer that so many wives have given me: he isn't treating her the way he did back then. After marriage, he thought he could do away with the preliminaries and get right to the main event. But it turns out that the "preliminaries" are important not only for a fulfilling sexual relationship but also in their own right.

In most cases, a woman needs to feel emotionally bonded with her husband before she wants to have sex with him. Sex for her becomes a physical expression of that emotional bond. She achieves this feeling through the exchange of affection and intimate conversation (chap. 4).

If you and your spouse are struggling sexually, a lack of affection may be your problem. Without the environment of affection, the sexual event feels contrived and unnatural for many women. All too often a wife may reluctantly agree to have sex with her husband even though she knows she won't enjoy it.

Most of the women I've counseled crave affection. I try to help their husbands understand the pleasure women feel when this need is met. It forms a vital part of a romantic relationship. Without it, a woman's sexual experience is incomplete.

Many husbands have this all backward. For them, sexual arousal makes them feel more affectionate. They try to explain to their wives the importance of having sex more often so that they'll feel like being more affectionate. But that argument usually falls on deaf ears. Some women *will* have sex with their husbands just for the affection they receive while making love, but it tends to leave them resentful and bitter. As soon as sex is over, their husbands go back to their unaffectionate ways, leaving their wives feeling unloved. They feel that all their husbands want is sex and that they don't really care about them in any other way. That attitude destroys their feeling of intimacy and the bond of unity. But that attitude can change if their husbands learn to create an environment of affection by learning habits that produce a steady stream of caring love.

QUESTIONS FOR HIM

1. On a scale of 1 to 10, with 10 being "very affectionate," how affectionate are you toward your wife? How would she rate you?
2. Is affection the environment for your entire marriage?
3. In the past, have you tended to equate affection with getting sexually aroused? Why hasn't this worked?
4. In what specific ways do you show your wife affection?
5. Would you be willing to have your wife coach you in how to show her more affection in the ways she really likes it?

QUESTIONS FOR HER

1. Is affection as important to you as this chapter claims?
2. If you're not getting enough affection from your husband, are you willing to coach him?
3. If making love is an emotional obstacle for you, would you find it easier to do if your husband was affectionate toward you?

TO CONSIDER TOGETHER

1. Is the topic of affection important enough to either of you to make changes?
2. How did you feel about Ted's assignment to become more affectionate to Paula? Would either of you find that assignment, or something similar to it, helpful?
3. What can you do to make affection mutually enjoyable?

FOUR

Intimate Conversation

When Julia and Nate were dating, it was just one long conversation. On days when they could not be together in person, they often talked on the phone, sometimes for an hour or more. They rarely planned formal dates because their real interest lay in seeing and talking with each other. Sometimes they got so busy talking that they forgot to do whatever they had planned for the evening.

But after they were married, Julia found that the frequency and the quality of her conversations with Nate declined sharply. He became involved in other things that took up more of his time. When they did have an opportunity to sit down and talk, Nate had less and less to say. When he came home from work, he generally spent time on his computer, watched sports on television, and went to bed early. To him, these changes did not mean he was disinterested in her or depressed about anything. He simply wanted to relax after a hard day at the office.

"Honey," Julia said one day, "I really miss our talks. I wish we could talk more like the way we used to."

"Yeah," Nate replied, "I enjoyed those times too. What would you like to talk about?"

That comment did not score as a deposit in Julia's Love Bank. She thought, "If you don't know the answer to that question, then I guess we don't have anything to talk about."

Why Won't My Husband Talk to Me?

I rarely hear a husband ask, "Why won't my wife talk to me more often?" but I often hear from wives, "Why is it so difficult for my husband to have a simple conversation with me?" Part of the answer to this last question is that men tend not to have as great a need for conversation as women. Most women enjoy conversation for its own sake. They will spend hours on the phone with other women, while men call other men less often just to chat and be brought up-to-date.

Why, then, does a man find it so easy to talk to a woman when they are dating? One obvious reason is that he wants to get to know her. First and foremost, he tries to understand her problems and how he can help; he wants to know what will make her happy and fulfilled.

Her personal history is also important to him. He asks questions about her family, her childhood, her greatest achievements and disappointments— and her past romantic relationships.

He also wants to learn how to be attractive to her. He calls and texts her whenever they can't be together because he knows that she likes that kind of attention. It shows her how much he cares about her and thinks of her.

But after marriage, especially after children arrive, he feels that he has learned enough about her and has proven his care for her. Since his need for conversation is usually much less than hers, he doesn't see any purpose in continuing to have the same long conversations they had while dating. He fails to understand that it was their conversations that helped trigger her feeling of love for him. By removing those conversations from their daily lives, he removes one of his most important sources of deposits into her Love Bank.

As I mentioned in the last chapter on affection, a woman wants to be with a man who cares deeply about her and for her. She wants assurances that he has caring love for her. When she perceives this kind of care expressed by his affection, she feels close to him. Since conversation is one of the most important ways that a man can communicate that care to a woman, conversation and affection are inseparably entwined. So just as affection should be a daily part of married life, intimate conversation should also continue daily.

What Makes a Conversation Intimate?

Julia wanted Nate to talk with her more often. But it wasn't just talk that she wanted. He could have started talking with her about almost anything, and she would have still been concerned. She wanted him to talk with her the *way* he did while they were dating. She wanted *intimate conversation*. While they were dating, his conversation had expressed his care for her. That's what made it intimate, and that's what made the conversation so enjoyable for her.

When people overhear typical conversations that my wife, Joyce, and I have, they know immediately that we care about each other. Many have told us that our tone of voice, the words we choose, and our body language all make it very obvious. It's true. We really do care for each other, and our conversation is a reflection of that care. For that reason, all our conversations with each other throughout the day are intimate conversations.

Affectionate acts that I discussed in the last chapter are expressions of caring love: hugging, kissing, and hand-holding are but a few of the ways that you and your spouse show your care for each other.

But care is best expressed in how a husband and a wife talk with each other. They communicate their caring love through their interest in each other, the topics they choose to discuss, and the words they use. When you hear it, intimate conversation is unmistakable. Julia knew that it had been quite a while since she had had an intimate conversation with Nate. That made her feel like he didn't care for her the way he had in the past.

The Friends of Intimate Conversation

All conversation in marriage should be intimate conversation because the way you talk with each other should reflect your care, regardless of the topic. But there are certain topics and ways to talk to each other that will make your care particularly evident. I call these the four friends of intimate conversation. Two describe the content and two describe the etiquette of intimate conversation.

Friend #1: Using Conversation to Inform, Investigate, and Understand Your Spouse

One of the most important purposes of marital conversation is to create emotional closeness. Nothing does this better than talking with each other in positive and encouraging ways. The more you learn about each other and the more you use that information to support each other, the more intimate your conversation becomes.

Inform each other of your emotional reactions, attitudes, opinions, daily experiences, and problems you may be facing. Answer every question honestly and respectfully. Provide information that your spouse wouldn't think to ask for. Keep calendars of your activities for the day and plans for your future and share them with each other. Tell your spouse your cell phone, social network, and email passwords, and don't erase anything until you have a chance to see each other's activity. Be completely transparent with each other. Don't keep any secrets.

Investigate, or get to know, each other's personal feelings and attitudes without being judgmental. Avoid making your questions seem like an interrogation. If you ever criticize or ridicule your spouse when they reveal personal information, they will be less likely to express it in the future. Instead, encourage each other to be open and vulnerable by being respectful and sensitive. One of the best ways to communicate care in marriage is to ask each other personal questions. It reflects your interest in each other.

Understand each other's emotional reactions—what makes you happy and sad and why it has that effect. Learn about each other's "hot" and "cold" buttons so that you can bring out the best in each other and avoid the worst. You demonstrate your care in marriage by responding to this understanding with changes in your behavior that promote pleasure and avoid pain for each other.

Friend #2: Developing an Interest in Each Other's Favorite Topics of Conversation

In my experience counseling couples, I have found that even the most introverted people become talkative when they discuss certain topics. Women may notice that their quiet husbands come out of their shells when out with a few male friends.

I once counseled a couple who was about to experience divorce. Jennifer could no longer accept Troy's silence. In my office, alone with me, he had no problem talking. However, when his wife joined us, he became stone quiet. What was his problem?

Certain topics of interest to him brought him out of his shell, and it didn't take me very long to figure out what they were. He was an absolute chatterbox when it came to those topics. Once those topics were introduced, he could then continue to converse about a wider range of other topics with me.

But because his wife was not willing to talk about anything that interested him, their conversation never got off the ground.

I encouraged her to become more educated about his favorite topic, which happened to be fishing. She not only learned about fish and fishing methods but also took the plunge and actually started fishing with him. What she thought would be very boring turned out to be enjoyable for her once she actually became educated about it.

At the same time, I encouraged him to pursue one of her interests, which was bird-watching. Fishing and bird-watching, activities they had been doing apart, actually came together to give them an enjoyable recreational activity they could do together.

The problem this couple faced was that they had failed to develop an interest in each other's favorite topics of conversation. The solution was to become more educated about those topics so that they could talk to each other creatively and intelligently.

Developing an interest in each other's favorite topics of conversation is an act of care. Your spouse's interests become your interests, and vice versa, because you want to be able to support each other in whatever you do.

Friend #3: Balancing the Conversation

Much has been written about being a good listener, but being a good talker is equally important. That's the reason the first friend I mentioned involved informing and investigating. You give information and receive information. Unless conversation is balanced in this way, it's a speech.

Amy and Ryan had a problem with conversation because she talked almost the entire time, while he sat and listened. I asked both of them to balance the amount of time they spoke. In a ten-minute conversation, she was to allow him about five minutes. At first, she expected him to say nothing during his time. But once she gave him a chance to talk, he filled his half of the ten minutes. Until she was required to balance their conversation, giving him an equal amount of time to speak, she remained unaware of her habit of dominating the conversation.

Some spouses ruin balance with the bad habit of interrupting. Before the other spouse can finish a thought, they break in with one of their own. Not only is this habit bad conversational etiquette, but it also prevents those who are somewhat restrained from remembering where their thought was taking them. Interruptions can put an end to an otherwise enjoyable conversation.

I encourage outgoing spouses to give their restrained partners a little more time to get their thoughts pulled together. Sometimes I encourage spouses to use two stopwatches to limit the amount of time each of them can speak (five minutes for each in a ten-minute conversation). This helps the outgoing spouse understand how much they tend to prevent the restrained spouse from speaking.

Those who monopolize conversation create an unwanted habit in their spouses—silence. Therefore, if you and your spouse want a good conversation, be sensitive to each other's right to "have the floor." It may take your spouse two or three seconds to begin a sentence, but allow whatever time is necessary. Also remember to wait until your spouse completes a thought before commenting on it.

Conversational balance reflects mutual care. A caring spouse values what the other has to say and are respectful of the time it takes to say it.

Friend #4: Giving Each Other Undivided Attention

One of the quickest ways for a husband to upset and offend his wife is to carry on a conversation with her while surfing the internet or responding to a text on his phone. She becomes upset because he is not paying close attention to what she is saying. He appears more interested in his phone. She's offended because she doesn't have his *undivided attention*.

Of course, husbands violate this rule of etiquette for much less absorbing reasons than the internet or a cell phone text. Many wives have complained to me that their husbands simply don't even try to listen to what they have to say. Some even fall asleep while their wives are talking.

Part of the reason that undivided attention is lacking in the conversation of so many couples is that the other friends of intimate conversation are missing. They are not talking about each other or about topics of interest. And the conversation is not balanced. Only the wife (or the husband) is doing the talking.

But that said, undivided attention requires practice, especially by men. A man should look into his wife's eyes while they are talking to each other—a sure indicator that he is giving her his attention.

As I discussed in chapter 2, "Romantic Relationships 101," I recommend that each week every married couple set aside fifteen hours for the purpose of giving each other their undivided attention. When I ask couples to document this time, I want a daily estimate from him and a daily estimate from her. Almost invariably, her estimate of the time they spent giving each other undivided attention is less than his. That's because women are usually more aware than men of what undivided attention really means.

Undivided attention reflects caring love. It's what you do when your spouse is your highest priority in life.

The Enemies of Intimate Conversation

Intimate conversation communicates caring love. It's safe and enjoyable. It's patient and kind. It makes Love Bank deposits. But anything that is said during a conversation that communicates selfishness rather than thoughtfulness expresses the opposite—I don't care about you.

When spouses talk to each other in an uncaring way, the enemies of intimate conversation have invaded their lives. This happens most often when spouses want to resolve a conflict in a selfish way.

Conversation in marriage *must* deal with conflicts. Joyce and I have a conflict almost every hour we are together: one of us wants to do something one way, and the other wants to do it a different way. But unless conflicts are resolved with mutual care that is safe and pleasant, conflicts are not usually resolved. Instead, they become one of the greatest sources of Love Bank withdrawals.

The trick to resolving conflicts the right way in marriage is to do it with the mutual caring love reflected in intimate conversation. But when selfishness rears its ugly head, the conversation is no longer intimate. It's adversarial. That's when the enemies of intimate conversation show up.

Spouses have such a tremendous effect on each other that two of the best questions they can ask each other are "What can I do to make you feel good today?" and "What have I done to make you feel bad?" That information can then be used to make more Love Bank deposits and fewer withdrawals in the future.

But when those questions are not specifically asked, I encourage spouses to reveal the answers in a nonjudgmental way. If my wife, Joyce, wants me to do something for her that will make her happy (meet her emotional need), I want to know about it. If something I do affects her negatively, I need to know about that too so that I can eliminate that behavior and do something pleasing to her instead. If she expresses her reactions to me as basic feelings rather than judgments, I don't feel at all defensive. But if she adds a judgment to her complaint, it makes me feel as if I'm being attacked. That brings out my defenses which makes resolving the problem much more difficult for me.

The enemies of intimate conversation turn what could have been a caring conversation into an unsafe and unpleasant conversation. They prevent couples from resolving their conflicts and expressing negative feedback in a caring and thoughtful way. These mistakes are a major source of Love Bank withdrawals.

Enemy #1: Making Demands

There's nothing wrong with you and your spouse asking for what you need from each other. I want you to understand and learn to meet each other's important emotional needs. But when your requests turn into demands, you've turned a corner that brings intimate conversation to a screeching halt.

Whenever you make a demand, you are telling your spouse you don't really care how they feel when they are fulfilling it. You want what you want, and that's all that matters. Of course, you may have fifty reasons why it's just and proper for your spouse to give you what you want or to resolve a conflict the way you want it resolved. But the bottom line is that you give your spouse no right to refuse. Demands don't communicate caring love. They communicate selfishness.

But they do more than that. Demands also make it *less likely* that you'll get what you want now or later. Even if you manage to force your spouse to obey your command this time, you can bet they will be on guard next time and attack fire with fire. Not only are demands enemies of intimate conversation, but they are also very foolish ways of trying to get what you may need, and may even deserve, in your marriage.

You may have legitimate needs that your spouse should be meeting for you. But the way you go about trying to get their attention will drive your spouse away if you make demands. They are threatening. *If you don't meet my demands, there will be consequences.*

A better approach to any marital problem is for either spouse to ask, "How would you feel about helping me with a problem I've been having?" This communicates care for your spouse, a willingness to negotiate, and an appeal to your spouse's care for you—essential elements of intimate conversation. Demands, on the other hand, communicate a lack of care.

Enemy #2: Being Disrespectful

A sure way to end intimate conversation is to say something that can be construed as being disrespectful and judgmental. Even something as simple as rolling your eyes in response to your spouse's comment can end what could have been a very enjoyable evening together. It's a lesson that some spouses never seem to learn.

Avoiding disrespect in marriage doesn't mean that you must agree with everything your spouse does or says. In fact, disagreements are to be expected in even the most successful marriages. But the way you disagree should not be offensive.

"But what if I don't respect my spouse's opinion," I often hear. "What should I say then?"

My answer has emotional and logical implications: *regardless of what you are thinking, don't say anything that's disrespectful.* Not saying anything that's disrespectful is an emotionally wise thing to do because disrespect is almost invariably offensive. It makes massive Love Bank withdrawals and usually cripples intimate conversation. Not saying something disrespectful is also a logical thing to do because disrespect prevents couples from finding solutions to their problems. Instead of the spouses searching for common ground, the discussion degenerates into a fight over differences in opinion or ends with the offended spouse walking away.

But sometimes spouses express disrespect with the goal of helping their spouse. They feel that their spouse's opinions and perspectives will get them into trouble someday. Being disrespectful is seen as an act of caring love. But even in such cases, disrespect will backfire. Instead of persuading your spouse, you will alienate them. Disrespect deals intimate conversation a fatal blow.

Since disrespect is so poorly understood, if there's ever a question about what makes a comment disrespectful, I have a simple way of answering it. If your spouse considers what you say to be disrespectful, it is.

Enemy #3: Expressing Anger

As damaging as they are to intimate conversation, demands and even disrespect can be innocent in intent. Spouses don't necessarily want to hurt each other when they engage those enemies—it just turns out that way.

But expressions of anger are always *intended* to be hurtful. Instead of caring love, uncaring hate is being expressed. Expressions of anger should have absolutely no place in marriage. They should never be tolerated.

So when spouses are angry with each other, they should say nothing until they've had a chance to cool off, because whatever they say will be abusive—and insane. Yes, insane. Take it from me, a clinical psychologist. When people are having an angry outburst, they are experiencing temporary insanity, and at the time they can be very dangerous. Instead of trying to protect, they are trying to attack and hurt the one who is the object of their anger, something spouses should never do to each other.

Angry outbursts have no place in any area of your life, but they are especially destructive in marriage. Your marriage should be a relationship of mutual protection and care. But anger turns you into your spouse's biggest threat. Whatever you might think of saying to your spouse when you're angry is better left unsaid. If you ever get a chance to see a video recording of one of your angry outbursts, you'll definitely agree with me.

Enemy #4: Dwelling on Mistakes, Past or Present

Mistakes are common in life, and they're especially common in marriage. Whenever we fail to take an opportunity to make our spouse happy or if we do something to make our spouse unhappy, we've made a mistake. But mistakes may be difficult to prove. What one person calls a mistake might seem correct or at least justifiable from another's perspective.

An affair is one of the biggest mistakes any spouse could make. The betrayed spouse would certainly regard it that way, but the unfaithful spouse would be unlikely to agree while the affair is happening and might not even see it that way after the affair is over. In fact, the unfaithful spouse would probably blame the betrayed spouse for the affair.

If it's difficult to establish blame for something as obviously wrong as an affair, can you imagine how difficult it is to establish blame for lesser offenses? And yet it's common for spouses to dwell on each other's mistakes and argue about who's to blame for their problems.

There's nothing wrong with expressing the fact that your spouse did something that offended you. In fact, I encourage it. The enemy that I'm referring to here is *dwelling* on the mistake. If you keep bringing it up, repeating it again and again, you will destroy intimate conversation.

If my wife, Joyce, tells me that I've done something that has offended her, I should accept her statement at face value. After all, she is the best judge of her own feelings. When she makes such a comment, she has revealed the impact of my behavior on her feelings. If I care for her feelings, I will want her to help me learn how to behave in a way that meets her needs. But if, after I accept her statement as true, she still dwells on my mistake, this makes me feel defensive. Instead of wanting to solve the problem, I want to avoid further discussion of the issue. That's why dwelling on mistakes is an enemy of intimate conversation.

I call the first three enemies of intimate conversation Love Busters, because that's what they do. Demands, disrespect, and anger destroy romantic love. In my book *Love Busters*, I explain how to avoid them and how to replace them with love-building alternatives.

It Takes Time to Talk

For a number of years, I studied couples who were dating, couples who had maintained romantic love while married, and couples who were having affairs. I was curious to know how they fell in love and what they did to maintain their romantic love. In all these cases, I found that those who maintained their love for each other *scheduled* time to talk to each other almost every day. During that time, regardless of what they were doing, they had each other's undivided attention, and they used much of it to engage in intimate conversation.

Based on these findings and overwhelming evidence I've acquired since then, I tell couples that if they want to maintain their love for each other, they should learn to do what those in love are doing—set aside time each day to engage in intimate conversation.

Without much time talking with their husbands, wives tend to lose the sense of intimacy they need so much. That loss greatly impacts their ability to enjoy sexual intimacy, the subject of the next chapter.

Conversation Tips for Husbands and Wives

As a caring husband, a man converses with his wife in a way that communicates his care for her. The way he talks to her and the topics he chooses to talk about all come together to create intimate conversation, an emotional need that she cannot do without.

Here is a list that summarizes essential aspects of intimate conversation. We've dealt with all of them. Now it's time to put them into action.

1. Use your conversation to inform, investigate, and understand each other.
2. Develop an interest in each other's favorite topics of conversation.
3. Balance your conversation. Learn to avoid interrupting each other and try to give each other the same amount of time to talk.
4. When you talk with each other, give each other undivided attention.
5. Never use conversation to force your spouse to do what you want or to agree with your way of thinking.

6. Never show disrespect for your spouse's feelings and opinions.

7. Never converse in anger.

8. Never use conversation to remind each other of past mistakes. Avoid dwelling on present mistakes as well.

When you meet your wife's need for intimate conversation, you come to understand each other more clearly and learn what it takes to meet other important emotional needs and resolve conflicts. Intimate conversation is essential if you want to be irresistible to each other.

QUESTIONS FOR HIM

1. Does the way you talk with your wife communicate your care for her? Do you talk to your wife about the problems she faces? Do you support her in trying to solve those problems? If not, why not?

2. Do you try to develop a better understanding of your wife's favorite topics of conversation? How can you improve?

3. Are you guilty of any of the enemies of intimate conversation? If so, how can you change? Can you see how they fail to communicate your care for her?

QUESTIONS FOR HER

1. Do you miss the quality of conversation you had while you were dating? If so, what can you do to help restore it?

2. Do you engage in any of the enemies of intimate conversation? If so, what can you do to avoid them in the future?

3. What interests do you and your husband have in common? What can you do to develop your understanding of his favorite topics of conversation?

TO CONSIDER TOGETHER

1. Do the enemies of intimate conversation prevent you from talking to each other as often as you should? If so, what can you do to eliminate them?

2. Do the friends of intimate conversation dominate the way you talk to each other? If not, what can you do to bring them on board?

3. How can you rearrange your schedules to make more time for intimate conversation? Would the time you currently spend doing something else be better spent with each other?

FIVE

Sexual Fulfillment

Before we married, Jim was so romantic and affectionate—a regular Don Juan. Now he seems more like Attila the Hun."

"When John wants sex, he wants it right now. He doesn't care how I feel; all he cares about is satisfying himself."

"Bob has turned into an animal. All he ever thinks about is sex, sex, sex!"

When I hear wives make remarks like these in my counseling office, I imagine how disillusioned they must feel. At one time, men who knew how to be affectionate and conversant swept these women off their feet. But once committed in marriage, all that vaporized, and what was left seemed like pure lust. Were the affection and conversation during the dating phase simply a ploy to win over a woman for sexual gratification?

"Why do you think your husband acts the way he does?" I ask.

"Because he doesn't really care about me. All he cares about is sex" is the usual answer—or words to that effect.

A mutually fulfilling marriage is a very conditional union: a union of mutual extraordinary care. If a husband does not try to meet his wife's needs, and she does not try to meet his, they may be legally married but they will not know the happiness and fulfillment marriage should provide. However, if both sides understand each other's needs and learn how to meet them, they will have the marriage they hoped for when they were first married.

I'm not trying to tell you what your most important emotional needs are or should be in marriage. You tell each other what your priorities are after you complete the Emotional Needs Questionnaire in appendix B and when you discuss the results together. In some cases, a husband and a wife will find that the most important needs I attribute to most men and women do not fit them. A husband may indicate a greater need for affection and intimate conversation than his wife. A wife may have a greater need for sexual fulfillment than her husband. I'm simply reflecting the way that thousands of men and women I've counseled have indicated to each other what they need the most in marriage. Wives have tended to report affection and intimate conversation as a higher priority in marriage than husbands. Husbands have tended to rank sexual fulfillment higher than their wives.

There is another point I've made that bears repeating: if one spouse ranks a certain need as a higher priority than the other spouse, that doesn't mean the other spouse doesn't have that need at all. It simply means that other needs are more important to that spouse.

What's the Difference?

There are three important differences between most men and women when it comes to sex. The first involves their sexual drive; the second, awareness of their sexuality; and the third, their primary reason to have sex.

Sexual Drive

The average man has a much higher sex drive than the average woman. This is because the only known aphrodisiac, testosterone, flows in abundance through men and is in much shorter supply in women. A woman can witness firsthand what an intense sex drive feels like by wearing a testosterone patch for a week to raise her level of the hormone to that of the average nineteen-year-old male. It's an eye-opening experience for women, who usually don't want to repeat it.

But over a lifetime, the level of testosterone in a man's bloodstream decreases about 1 percent a year, which makes him less sexually motivated and less able to perform as he ages. For this reason, older men don't necessarily rank sexual fulfillment as important as they did earlier in life.

Sexual Awareness

The second difference between most men and women is their awareness of their sexuality. I use the term *sexual awareness* to convey an understanding of one's own sexual experience—knowledge of how to respond sexually. Over the years, I have collected more than forty thousand questionnaires from clients that ask about their sexual history and sexual behavior. Based on the results of these questionnaires, it is apparent that almost all men masturbate, and many start at a very young age (eight to ten). On the other hand, girls who masturbate begin much later, most often in their late teens and early twenties, and more than half of the women surveyed never masturbate at all.

The first heterosexual experiences reported by the men and women surveyed took place at essentially the same ages (between thirteen and sixteen). But their reports of that experience differed remarkably. Almost every man surveyed enjoyed his first heterosexual encounter, while most women reported finding it to be a disappointment.

I believe at least part of this discrepancy lies in the differences between men's and women's sex drives. For the most part, boys are greatly helped by a strong sex drive and a history of sexual responsiveness through masturbation, while girls do not often come to that first encounter with much of a sexual history at all. Many do not know what to expect. A desire to be liked by their boyfriend or curiosity motivates them, but maybe not the feeling of an urgent need for sexual gratification. "What is the big deal about sex, anyway?" they often ask.

This disparity in terms of sex drive and experience lies at the root of many marital problems. Young men and women often come together in marriage from opposite ends of the spectrum. Perhaps he is more sexually experienced and motivated by strong desires; perhaps she is less experienced and less motivated. Furthermore, his experience is so visceral and almost automatic that he usually does not understand that most women must learn how to respond sexually, and he is not prepared to talk to his bride about enjoying her own sexuality. He just knows how much he loves it and assumes that what he enjoys must feel as good to her. Most young husbands discover the falsehood of that assumption before very long; they learn the frustrating truth that the wonderful sexual discoveries they have made seem much less meaningful to their brides. For many men, this becomes a source of unparalleled frustration.

Most men cannot achieve complete sexual fulfillment in marriage unless their wives are also sexually fulfilled. While I have maintained that men typically need sex more than women, unless a woman joins her husband in the sexual experience, his need for sex usually remains unmet. Therefore, a woman does her husband no favors by sacrificing her body to his sexual advances. He can feel sexually satisfied only when she joins him in the experience of lovemaking.

The same is true for the fulfillment of affection and intimate conversation in women. Wives don't usually feel fulfilled by their husbands' affection and intimate conversation unless they are also fulfilled by the experience. They must enjoy it too. That's why the concept of mutuality is so important in the meeting of all emotional needs. Even though one spouse may have the greater need, it can be met effectively only if both spouses are fulfilled.

But I've counseled many wives who are fully aware of their own sexuality and have no problem enjoying sex yet refuse to make love to their husbands. They tell me that they can become sexually aroused and reach a climax, often responding faster than their husbands do. Yet they won't do it. This common problem is due to the third difference between most men and women—their primary reason to have sex.

Sexual Motivation

A very important question to ask your spouse is "Why should we make love?" If the husband is honest, he will answer with something to the effect that making love relieves his sexual craving. But the answer of most wives is very different. A wife might say that sex validates an existing closeness and helps her feel closer to her husband. For her, it is more about intimacy and emotional bonding.

So if a wife doesn't feel emotionally close to her husband, she usually won't want to make love to him. He has probably failed to communicate his caring love for her with affection and intimate conversation, or he's proven that he really doesn't care by ignoring her completely—until he feels like having sex. Women who are emotionally withdrawn from their husbands are often unwilling to have sex with them. Husbands, on the other hand, rarely turn down an opportunity to have sex with their wives, even when they feel totally disconnected.

Understanding these three differences in the sexuality of men and women allows couples to be able to logically address just about any sexual problem they face. Negotiation begins with a respectful exchange of perspectives, and by discussing these differences with each other and searching for ways to make sex fulfilling for both of you, you and your spouse will be able to find a solution to one of the most common problems in marriage.

How to Achieve Sexual Compatibility

Let's review once more the three important differences between men and women when it comes to sex.

1. *Sexual drive*. The abundance of the aphrodisiac hormone, testosterone, in men and much less of it in women gives men a much greater craving for sex.
2. *Sexual awareness*. Boys tend to explore their sexuality earlier and more often than girls. By the time men marry, they may have a better understanding of how to have a gratifying sexual experience.
3. *Sexual motivation*. Because men have a much higher sex drive, the primary reason they have sex is to relieve their craving. For women, the primary reason is often intimacy and emotional bonding.

To help couples develop sexual compatibility in their marriage, I address all three of these important differences as I present a quick lesson in human sexuality. While some of this material may seem a bit unromantic and clinical, bear with me. The better you understand the following information, the better you can meet each other's needs sexually.

Most sexual conflicts are resolved when a husband and a wife learn what actually happens—emotionally and physiologically—when they make love to each other. The sexual experience can be divided into five stages: willingness, arousal, plateau, climax, and recovery.

The first stage, *willingness*, gets the ball rolling. The husband's willingness is usually motivated by sexual desire, while the wife is usually motivated by her emotional connection to him. During *arousal*, he and she begin to sense sexual feelings. His penis usually becomes erect, and her vagina secretes lubricating fluid. If his penis glans and her clitoris are stimulated properly through intercourse or manual stimulation, the husband and wife pass into the *plateau* stage. In this stage, his penis becomes very hard and her vagina contracts involuntarily, providing greater resistance and a heightened sensation during intercourse. The *climax*, which lasts only a few seconds, is the peak of the sexual experience. At this time, the penis ejects semen in bursts (ejaculation), and the vagina alternately contracts and releases several times. The *recovery* period follows in which both partners feel peaceful and relaxed; the penis becomes soft, and the vagina, no longer secreting lubricating fluid, relaxes.

While men and women experience the same five stages, they do not usually do so in the same physical and emotional ways. What works for most men does not work for most women. What works for most women does not work for most men. Couples who wish to experience sexual compatibility need to appreciate and understand the differences. I will discuss each stage of the sexual response separately and highlight some of the most important differences.

Willingness—How It All Starts

I have already said that most men are motivated to have sex because of a sexual craving created by their relatively high level of testosterone. Women, on the other hand, are more often motivated by emotional closeness. Many men experience the craving for sex almost daily, which may not happen as often for women. So men are generally willing to have sex whenever their wives offer it because of ongoing sexual desire. But most women are willing to have sex as often as their husbands offer it only if they feel emotionally close to them.

The reason most women are willing to have sex with their husbands is that they want to express their love for them in this way. They want to extend their affection, which is the expression of their caring love, into lovemaking. That's the reason affection and intimate conversation create the *environment* that makes the *event* of sex attractive to most women.

There's another reason a woman is willing to make love: she anticipates a mutually enjoyable sexual experience with her husband. That's possible only if he understands how she can enjoy the remaining four stages of the sexual experience and applies that understanding to their lovemaking.

In most cases, an environment of affection and intimate conversation and the anticipation of a mutually enjoyable sexual experience result in a woman's willingness to make love to her husband whenever he has a sexual desire.

Arousal—the Beginning of Sexual Feelings

Most men can become sexually aroused in a variety of ways, but the hands-down favorite is visual. Numerous magazines, calendars, films, videos, and so on that feature nude or barely clad women all cash in on one thing: men like to look at naked women. During counseling sessions, wives readily testify that their husbands enjoy watching them undress and that when they are naked, their husbands' arousal follows in just a few seconds.

Most men experience arousal easily, and it may happen several times a day for young men. Many nonvisual and visual experiences can do it: a scent of perfume in an elevator, watching a woman's walk, looking at a photo of a scantily clad woman, or even daydreaming.

Sometimes a wife expresses dismay at her husband's ability to be sexually aroused by other women. But she needs to understand that her husband is not being promiscuous or unfaithful. He is simply experiencing a characteristic male reaction. Arousal in itself doesn't mean that much to most men. It may occur relatively effortlessly, and they sometimes experience it whether or not they want to. Women may find this hard to understand because they can experience arousal so differently than men do. Much more complicated and deliberate, a woman's excitement does not, in most cases, depend on visual stimulation.

For most men, sexual willingness and sexual arousal come together so effortlessly that they don't consider them to be two separate stages. For most women, however, the two are quite different. Arousal usually doesn't take place unless there is a deliberate decision to let it happen.

If a woman is willing to make love, she will usually encourage her husband to touch her in ways that lead to her arousal. But if she's not willing, the same touching usually leads to a very defensive and angry reaction. In other words, *only* her willingness gives him the right to do what it takes to arouse her sexually.

Once a woman is willing to be aroused, she's ready to receive and respond to appropriate tactile stimulation, such as the caressing of her body (especially the breasts and nipples) and stimulation of the area surrounding the clitoris. I usually encourage a couple to avoid intercourse until the woman is sexually aroused. By then, her vagina is well-lubricated, and the risk of an uncomfortable entry is greatly reduced. She is also more responsive to intercourse when she is aroused.

When intercourse begins, a woman needs to sustain strong stimulation to her clitoris and vaginal opening. She learns to create this more intensive stimulation by (1) contracting her pubococcygeus (PCG) muscle (it is the muscle used to stop urine flow), which tightens the vagina on the inserted penis; (2) thrusting her pelvis rapidly; (3) and assuming a position that increases pressure on the clitoris and resistance to the penis in the vaginal opening.

The shorter the distance between a woman's clitoris and the tip of her vaginal opening, the easier it is for her to be sexually stimulated through intercourse. A distance less than one-half inch generally makes stimulation almost effortless, while a distance of more than one inch can be challenging. But those with a clitoris-vagina distance greater than one inch can find intercourse to be a very satisfying sexual experience if they experiment with various positions until they find one that works for them. When they find that position, their husbands should not try to deviate from it.

As I implied earlier, if a husband wants his wife to truly feel cared for and be a willing sex partner, he should guarantee that each sexual experience is enjoyable for her. So she should be able to tell him what he can do to achieve that objective, and he should do it for her. Sexual positions and techniques should be limited to ones they both enjoy. Usually that means discovering what she enjoys most and sticking to it.

With lovemaking in mind, I highly recommend that spouses be affectionate while becoming sexually aroused. It's not just sex. It's a bonding experience, especially for most women. So spouses should kiss each other, hug each other, and look at each other. If the way you have sex prevents you from being affectionate, it ceases to be lovemaking.

Plateau—the Best Stage of Lovemaking

A few minutes of intense physical stimulation usually bring an aroused man and woman to the next stage—the sexual plateau. In arousal, a soft penis must be voluntarily hardened, and a loose vagina must be voluntarily tightened to have the best effect. But in the plateau stage, the penis is hard and the vagina is tight involuntarily. A man can't relax his penis, and a woman can't loosen her vagina. The sexual pleasure experienced in this stage is intense and can be maintained for extended periods of time.

While women need very special and intense stimulation to reach a plateau, men need much less stimulation. Intercourse itself is almost always sufficient for men, and many reach a plateau with even less stimulation.

Unfortunately, a woman's need for more stimulation and a man's need for less create a common sexual problem: premature ejaculation, which means that he comes to a climax too soon. As she thrusts quickly to stimulate herself to the plateau, the stimulation becomes too great for him. He experiences a climax and loses his erection before she can reach a plateau or climax.

On the other hand, if a man tries to hold back a climax, he may find himself falling from the plateau stage back to arousal, and his penis softens. Although he may continue intercourse, his penis is not hard enough to give his wife the stimulation she needs unless he voluntarily keeps it hard.

For many men, maintaining the plateau stage without rising to a climax or receding to arousal is a challenge. When having intercourse, the husband should hold the plateau about ten minutes, the time his wife needs to reach the plateau. Then she may need another five minutes to experience a climax. But men commonly climax before their wives have enough stimulation to enjoy the plateau or reach climax. So even the best-intentioned man needs training to achieve this goal.

Recent advances in medical science that help men maintain a hard erection have been very successful. While these medications were originally designed for aging men who had developed impotence (failure to maintain an erection), men as young as twenty-five are now finding that these medications help them create a consistently enjoyable sexual experience. I have recommended these medications to many of my clients who have had problems maintaining a hard erection during intercourse.

Climax—Ecstasy or Anxiety?

Many consider the climax (or orgasm) an ecstatic experience that both partners should try to reach simultaneously for optimal pleasure. Because of this popular idea, many people have a distorted view of the climax, and some couples, in an effort to reach their goal of climaxing together, lose out on the pleasure of the entire lovemaking experience. When a couple feels anxiety rather than an enjoyment of each other, they are putting too much importance on performance and not enough on the pleasure of their lovemaking.

The woman who knows how to reach a plateau is only one small step away from reaching a climax; it takes only a little more time and stimulation. However, some women I've counseled have confided in me that they really don't find reaching a climax worth the effort it takes to do so. They have reached it at times, but they are quite happy with the sex act without a climax and wish their husband would not try to pressure them to achieve it. In my practice, I have observed that women with an abundance of energy usually choose to climax whenever they make love. In fact, they often choose to climax many times while making love. Women with less energy or women who feel tired after a long, hard day often choose not to climax. Men, on the other hand, whether full of energy or exhausted, almost always choose to climax because it requires such little additional effort.

A good sexual relationship takes this difference of effort into account. A caring man will not put pressure on his wife to climax because he realizes she may enjoy sex more without it. Anxiety over whether or not to climax has no place in a fulfilling sexual relationship.

Recovery—Afterglow or Resentment?

An appropriate description of the recovery phase is an afterglow, with both partners lying in each other's arms feeling completely fulfilled. But because men and women do not share the same instincts after a climax, this ideal state eludes many couples.

Characteristically, following a climax, a woman falls back into the plateau stage and can reach another climax if she so chooses. If she does not decide to climax again, she slowly falls back to arousal and then finally to an unaroused level. As this takes place, she feels a deep sense of peace come over her and generally has a deep desire for continuing affection. Many women I counsel report that this feeling may remain for up to an hour after intercourse.

During the recovery period, most men do not experience the same feelings. A second climax for men is not as desirable because it requires much more effort than the first, if a man can achieve it at all. For most men, a third climax within a short period of time is nearly impossible. Unlike the woman, the man does not fall back to the plateau after climax. He usually falls back into arousal, and even that is short-lived. Within minutes of a climax, many men are totally uninterested in sex. Often, such men will jump up and take a shower or roll over and go to sleep. Many a honeymoon has been destroyed by such insensitive behavior.

Each couple must work out for themselves a proper sense of timing at the recovery stage. A man should be ready to bring his wife to another sexual climax through digital stimulation if she chooses, or he should continue showing her affection for at least fifteen to twenty minutes. Don't let this warm and meaningful time for conversation escape you.

On the other hand, a wife should try not to take her husband's sudden loss of sexual interest as a rejection of her. She needs to understand that the purely physical part of his sex drive rises after a period of physical abstinence and falls shortly after a climax. This does not mean that he no longer loves her, despite the fact that his sex drive has momentarily hit a low point. If he remains affectionate during the recovery period, he proves that his care for her is not just about sex.

Solving Sexual Problems

While sexual problems cause tension and unhappiness in many marriages, these difficulties can be solved more easily than one might think. In most cases, solving them merely requires education. In regard to such problems, spouses willing to learn what they need to know and to practice it together will achieve fulfillment. Many ask me, "How do we get educated?"

You are each other's best teachers. Learn from each other's reactions. Make your learning experience pleasant and safe. Never force each other to do anything that is unpleasant for either of you. If your sexual experiences reflect your mutual extraordinary care, you will discover sexual techniques that no book or course can teach you.

If you encounter any pain or discomfort during intercourse, or if you experience a sudden drop in sexual interest, a urologist or gynecologist can often help by examining possible physical causes and providing medical solutions. As I've said earlier, avoid any sexual experience that is painful or even unpleasant. Sex should be mutually enjoyable.

One of the tragic ironies of my job appears when I counsel couples in their seventies for sexual incompatibility. Almost always they resolve their problem within a few weeks, and many experience sexual fulfillment for the first time after forty or fifty years of marriage. "What a difference this would have made in our marriage," they often report. While I am happy that they have finally resolved a long-standing and frustrating marital problem, I feel sad for the years they unnecessarily endured the guilt, anger, and depression that often accompany sexual incompatibility.

Sexual Aversion

A tragic consequence of a spouse forcing sex on an unwilling spouse (marital rape) is sexual aversion. It is a very real physical and emotional reaction that is usually very painful and can cause the victim to experience intense pain, nausea, and vomiting. All of us have a negative reaction to being forced to do what we choose not to do, but when it comes to sex, the negative reaction is often disabling.

When a couple comes to my office for help with their sexual relationship, I often find the wife experiencing a sexual aversion—whether as a result of marital rape or something different. It is a very negative reaction to any and all forms of sex. While sometimes the reaction is purely physical, it is often also emotional. For many of these women, and for some men, having sex is an absolute nightmare.

Sometimes a sexual aversion is not entirely the fault of the husband. Because the wife may feel obligated to have sex, she may put herself through whatever her husband finds enjoyable without complaining—until the pain is too great to ignore.

If sex is painful or unpleasant for either of you, stop making love immediately and discuss what might be going wrong. Don't begin again until the source of the problem is identified and solved. If you correct the problem before an aversion begins to develop, you will be back to making love with mutual enjoyment very quickly. But if you wait for an aversion to develop, it may take weeks or even months to return to normal lovemaking while you are extinguishing the aversive reaction with relaxation techniques and pleasurable experiences.

The Policy of Sexual Exclusivity

When comparing any two experiences, the most enjoyable one will make the other one seem boring. Psychologists call this the "contrast effect." So when it comes to having sex, one of the best ways to enjoy each other is to rid yourselves of the competition. When a spouse tells me that sex in marriage is boring, I immediately suspect there are competing forms of sex, usually pornography or even an affair. But a host of other forms of non-marital sex can also enter your lives. So I've created a rule to help couples keep their lovemaking vibrant. I call it the Policy of Sexual Exclusivity.

> **Never engage in any sexual act or experience that does not include your spouse.**

Pornography is a couple's greatest risk because it gives viewers a completely false impression of what sex should be and who it should be with. If all of a couple's sexual experiences, including masturbation, are with each other, their sexual attractiveness to each other will remain solid. But if the images of others fog their thinking, sex with each other will tend to be unfulfilling.

Sexual Reluctance in Husbands

As I repeat throughout this book, not everyone has the typical needs of the "average" man or woman. An emotional need that I describe as being characteristic of most men can, in some cases, be a woman's most important emotional need. Many times it's actually the wife who craves sex, and it's the husband who is reluctant. In those cases, the three differences in sexuality between most men and women merit close analysis. When a husband is reluctant to make love, it's usually because one or more of these differences do not characterize the couple.

Generally, I begin with an analysis of the first difference, sexual drive. Has the husband's level of testosterone dropped to a point where he no longer has a craving for sex? If so, a testosterone supplement can solve the problem. Many of my clients who are over fifty have chosen this solution to increase their sexual interest.

Another factor that affects sex drive for men is masturbation. Since most men experience a greatly reduced sex drive after a climax, men who masturbate even occasionally will often show less interest in marital sex. That's one of the reasons I warn men to avoid any sexual experience—especially pornography—that does not involve their wives. If a man's wife is his only source of sexual gratification, he is usually motivated to have sex with her as frequently as she wants.

The second difference, sexual awareness, can sometimes be the culprit. Because sex is so effortless for most young men, they will often assume that their sexual response will be available to them throughout life. Then as they age, they find they have difficulty sustaining their arousal and become impotent, which means they lose their erection while making love. Instead of having a predictably enjoyable experience, they suffer the indignity of sexual failure. This failure, in turn, creates an understandable sexual reluctance.

Medication to improve sexual performance is one solution to this problem. But another solution for these men is to do what I recommend for most women. Try different positions and sexual techniques until you find one that is predictably effective in triggering a sexual response.

The third difference, sexual motivation, can also play a role in either spouse's sexual reluctance. A fight can ruin a desire for sex for many men, even when their sex drive is functioning normally. And many couples fight daily. A man who wants sex for the same reason most women do—to have an intimate and emotionally bonding experience—would not want to make love when his wife is demanding, disrespectful, or angry. He wants to run for cover.

An analysis of a husband's sexual reluctance may reveal problems with his sexual drive, sexual awareness, and/or sexual motivation. Once that analysis is completed, the solution to his problem can be identified and implemented. It should be just as incumbent for a husband to meet his wife's need for sexual fulfillment as it is for a wife to meet her husband's need.

The Marital Golden Rule

Almost all cultures and ages know the Golden Rule. Jesus Christ taught us, "Do to others as you would have them do to you" (Luke 6:31). As you think about the concepts presented so far and look ahead to the other seven emotional needs, please consider this slight revision of the Golden Rule:

> Meet your spouse's emotional needs as you would want your spouse to meet yours—with quality, quantity, and mutuality.

The care that's provided between a husband and wife isn't usually the same because the needs of a husband and a wife are not usually the same. Your expression of extraordinary care is reflected in your meeting of needs that are important to one of you but not necessarily as important to the other.

QUESTIONS FOR HER

1. Do the three primary differences in sexuality between men and women apply to you and your husband? Have you addressed these differences to create a mutually fulfilling sexual experience?
2. Does your husband act like he is entitled to have sex with you because he made a commitment to have an exclusive sexual relationship with you? If yes, have you ever shared with him how his feeling of self-imposed entitlement may be causing lovemaking to be an unpleasant experience or something you avoid and what needs of yours that means he's dismissing?
3. While reading this chapter, did you learn anything about you and your husband that you did not already know?

QUESTIONS FOR HIM
---

1. Do the three primary differences in sexuality between men and women apply to you and your wife? Have you addressed these differences to create a mutually fulfilling sexual experience?
2. Do you feel entitled to have sex with your wife because you have made a commitment to have an exclusive sexual relationship with her? Has that feeling of entitlement ever kept you from doing what it takes to motivate her to make love more often (to be more affectionate and make the experience more enjoyable for her)?
3. According to this chapter, a woman is aroused by her husband's affection, attentiveness, warmth, kindness, and tender sensitivity. Do you consistently try to develop and express these qualities? What do you think your wife would say in answer to this question?

TO CONSIDER TOGETHER
---

1. Discuss your answers to the previous questions with each other.
2. On a scale of 1 to 10, with 10 being "very satisfactory," how would each of you rate the five stages of your sexual response? willingness ___ arousal ___ plateau ___ climax ___ recovery ___
3. If you rated any of the five steps fairly low, what do you think can be done to overcome the problem?
4. "I warn men to avoid any sexual experience—especially pornography—that does not involve their wives" (p. 77). There are many reasons for this warning. Think of a few. Do you agree or disagree? Share with each other how you feel about this statement.
5. The workbook *Five Steps to Romantic Love* contains the Sexual Experience Inventory, the Strategy to Discover the Five Stages of Sexual Experience, the Sexual Fulfillment Inventory, the Strategy to Meet the Need of Sexual Fulfillment, and the Sexual Fulfillment Worksheet. To help you communicate your sexual experiences to each other and create a mutually enjoyable sexual experience, you should complete these worksheets.

SIX

Recreational Companionship

H i, Cindy, this is Alan."

"Hello! How nice of you to call." Her voice sounded warm and cheerful.

"I have tickets for the Bruins-Bears game at the Rose Bowl on Saturday. Would you like to go with me?"

"That sounds great! What time?"

They made the date, and Alan smiled after he hung up. He and Cindy had gone out twice in the four weeks they had known each other. This would be the first "sports date," and he was pleased that she sounded so eager to go.

They had a great time at the game. Cindy seemed to understand enough about football to know what was happening, and they even discussed some of the plays afterward at the coffee shop.

That autumn they took in several more games in addition to a half dozen movies. Cindy's taste in films pleased Alan too, and the romance was progressing nicely. By midwinter, Alan felt convinced he had found the right girl—at last. The weekend his car broke down doubly confirmed it in his mind. He called Cindy to explain.

"Honey, I'm sorry. My car won't run, and I have to try to fix it this afternoon to have it for work on Monday."

"Oh, that's okay. Why don't I get my roommate to run me over and I'll give you a hand? I'll bring coffee and sandwiches."

The car repair turned into one of their best dates ever. Cindy handed Alan tools, and they worked together while talking about some of the latest car models.

This girl, thought Alan, *is really special.*

They arranged their wedding for the first week in May. On their honeymoon, they went to the mountains to do a little hiking together. The summer passed blissfully with some trips to the beach, and everything went very well—until football season. At the last minute, Cindy begged off on going with Alan to see UCLA play Arizona State. By the end of the season, she had attended only two games with him. So one night at dinner, early in December, Alan brought this turn of events to Cindy's attention. "I thought you liked football," he complained.

"Oh, honey, I do. I guess I just don't enjoy it quite as much as you do. A couple of games during the season are enough for me," she replied.

"Oh," said Alan flatly, not sure how to handle this new and unexpected information.

"I've been meaning to ask you about something," she continued. "The county art museum has a special exhibit of Spanish Renaissance paintings this month. Would you go with me?"

"Yeah, sure, I guess so," Alan replied.

Over the next year, Alan discovered that the things he liked to do and the things Cindy *really* liked to do had little in common. Her interest in cars had evaporated practically overnight, and he felt lucky to get her to even one football game. Meanwhile, she insisted that he take her to more art museums and an occasional concert or opera. Gradually, they arrived at the point where they rarely did much together except go out to dinner once in a while.

At the end of two years of marriage, they had an agreement that he would spend an evening or an afternoon each week going to sporting events with his friends, and she would do what she enjoyed most with her friends. Alan would have preferred to spend more "fun" time with Cindy, but she seemed quite content with the arrangement.

Hurt and bewildered, Alan often asked himself, *I wonder what made her change?*

How Important Is Recreational Compatibility?

In counseling sessions, I have heard many variations of Cindy and Alan's experience. Of course, Cindy never really "changed." It is not uncommon for women or men, when they are single, to join someone they are attracted to in pursuing that person's interests. They find themselves doing a variety of activities and perhaps watching movies they never would have chosen on their own.

But after marriage, spouses are usually less likely to engage in activities that are not enjoyable to them. They don't feel that it's necessary anymore, because they no longer need these activities as a way of getting together.

One spouse may try to interest the other in those pre-marriage activities, but if their attempts fail, they often find themselves engaging in them alone or with someone else. Their spouse usually encourages it.

Men usually place a surprising amount of importance on recreational activities. When men are dating, recreational compatibility is usually a crucial criterion for them, and they assume that their future bride will become their lifelong recreational companion. In most cases, a woman's interest in a man's favorite activities helps make enough Love Bank deposits to seal the marriage deal.

So if a wife announces after marriage that she's no longer interested in joining her husband in his favorite activities and that he should enjoy them with his friends instead, it usually comes as a shock. It also eliminates one of the most important ways that she makes Love Bank deposits.

Most men treasure the time they spend recreationally. They plan for it, look forward to it, and will often spend quite a bit of money making it especially enjoyable. The TV stereotypes showing husbands out with the guys on fishing trips saying "It doesn't get any better than this" make that point. But my counseling files prove that it *can* get a lot better than that if a husband's favorite recreational companion is his wife. In fact, among the ten most important emotional needs in marriage, spending recreational time with his wife is ranked second only to sex for the typical husband. It's so important that I consider it to be a need that *must* be met to sustain his feeling of love in marriage.

People may challenge my claim, saying they know any number of happily married couples whose recreational interests are totally different. But these people do not necessarily know the couples in their most honest moments. I have counseled married couples who maintained an excellent image right up to the moment of divorce. They successfully hid their deepest needs from themselves and others until it was too late.

Sometimes recreational tastes overshadow deep, personal needs. By nature, men and women seem to have divergent tastes when it comes to having fun. Many men enjoy recreational activities that involve more risk, more adventure, and more violence than women enjoy. Typically, men pursue such sports as football, boxing, hunting, fishing, hang gliding, scuba diving, snowmobiling, and skydiving. They tend to prefer movies with sex and violence and may not mind sweat, dirt, body odor, or belching during a recreational activity. Many women find some or all of these things unpleasant and tasteless.

Women statistically prefer to engage in quieter activities, such as watching romantic movies, going to cultural events, going out to lunch or dinner, dancing, and shopping. They tend to put less emphasis on the activity itself and more emphasis on the social interaction. The one they are with is usually more important than what they are doing. For most women, a good conversation can be a recreational event.

The classic, stereotypical struggle finds the woman trying to "clean up the man's act," making him shave, dress more neatly, talk more gently, and so on. When she moves in on his recreational life, he may conclude that she wants to spoil one of the only things that keeps him going in life. He still loves her, but she begins to cramp his style. To avoid that, he spends an increasing amount of time with men only. This allows him to do what he enjoys most without restraint. But it also means that his most enjoyable activities are done without his wife present. And an opportunity for her to make huge Love Bank deposits is lost.

Growing Apart

In our opening story, Alan was disappointed and wondering why Cindy had changed. In some marriages, a man like Alan would just trudge off alone to watch his Bruin Gridders and make the best of it. But what happened to Alan is all too common. He joined a softball league with some of his buddies, where he met Hillary, who just loves sports of all kinds. They had a cup of coffee as they shared baseball trivia, and before they knew it, they had become good friends. (After all, softball leagues last for months.)

If Alan isn't careful, he will find himself in an affair with Hillary, who promises to meet all the recreational needs Alan expects Cindy to meet. He doesn't recognize his susceptibility to Love Bank deposits made through recreational activities. As a result, he does not establish boundaries to guard his Love Bank. If the story plays out to its ironic end, Alan will divorce Cindy to marry Hillary and—you guessed it—*she* might suddenly decide that concerts, or maybe shopping, are more fun than baseball or football. I have seen this exact irony come back to haunt men who thought an affair, divorce, and remarriage would solve their problems.

I must emphasize that spouses with this primary need don't usually wander into an affair out of anger or revenge. Alan felt hurt by Cindy's change of behavior, but he didn't begrudge her the right to revert to her real interests. The danger in all of this lies in the two of them simply continuing to grow further and further apart. That common pattern at its worst can lead to an affair and divorce; the wise couple will avoid this trend in their marriage or correct it as soon as it begins.

It Happened to Me Too

I understand the confusion Alan and other husbands like him face when their wives start to retreat from recreational activities they once enjoyed together. I've been there. For example, when I was younger, I loved to play chess. I started at age four and eventually became president of the university club, where I was first board.

After I married, I gave up chess tournaments because Joyce didn't play and had no interest in learning. Chess is an extremely time-consuming game to pursue, and as much as I loved it, I decided we could better spend our recreational time doing something we both enjoyed. I thought we would both enjoy tennis, since we had spent countless hours playing during our courtship days. But during the first year of marriage, Joyce announced,

"Bill, I don't really enjoy tennis that much anymore. I think I would prefer other ways of spending time together."

Joyce's turnaround on tennis came as a complete surprise to me. We had dated for six years before we married, and I thought she enjoyed tennis as much as I did. I didn't realize that she played it just to be with me. But after we were married, she reasoned, we'd be together without having to do things she didn't enjoy. So early in our marriage, she did the right thing. She let me know that tennis wasn't her favorite activity and that she'd rather we do something else together.

This was a very important choice point for me in our marriage. I could have done what many spouses do—continue to play tennis with someone else. At the time, Joyce would probably have gone along with that solution, as long as my new partner was my friend Steve.

But I didn't make that decision. Instead, I chose a different path. I forgot about tennis and found a new activity that Joyce and I could enjoy together. We switched from tennis to volleyball and played on the same team. And we expanded our interests in movies, plays, concerts, dining out, exercising, sightseeing, and enjoying nature.

Because we stayed together in pursuit of recreation, today we spend almost all our recreational time with each other. The outcome could have been quite different if I had stuck to tennis and chess and let Joyce go her way. We would have grown apart, each experiencing our most enjoyable moments of fun and relaxation without the other.

When I counsel married couples, I can't emphasize too strongly what a mistake it can be for spouses to have separate primary recreational activities. Instead of making steady deposits into each other's Love Bank by having fun together, they miss a golden opportunity. They spend some of their most enjoyable moments in the company of *someone else*, with the distinct possibility of building a Love Bank account with that person. When spouses are not each other's favorite recreational companion, not only do they risk losing their love for each other, but they also risk falling in love with whoever turns out to be their opposite sex companion.

If you want to have a fulfilling marriage, your favorite recreational companion *must* be your spouse.

How to Find Mutual Recreational Interests

When I explain the importance of mutual recreational interests to couples in my office, some have no problem discovering things to do together. Others, however, are at a total loss. "They are just too different," they claim. "And besides, he simply won't give up his golf." Or "She absolutely must continue her book club on Tuesday afternoons."

In response to their pessimistic attitude, I told them to imagine that around each of them is drawn an invisible circle encompassing all their recreational interests and sources of enjoyment. There are thousands of them—some they know about, and some they have yet to discover. Within their two circles, there are hundreds of recreational interests that overlap—they both enjoy doing them. Again, they may vaguely know about some of them, but almost all are still a mystery. From the hundreds of overlapping interests, they need to find only a few because they won't have time for all of them. Once they find, say, five or ten activities that they both enjoy doing together and they spend all their recreational time together, they'll become each other's favorite recreational companion."

To discover these overlapping recreational interests, I encourage the couple to complete my Recreational Enjoyment Inventory (a copy can be found in appendix C). It's a list of more than 100 recreational activities with space to indicate how much a husband or a wife likes or dislikes each one. Ratings are from -3 (very unpleasant) to +3 (very enjoyable). Couples can add activities to the list and rate them as well. When the list is completed, it may include as many as 130 activities, each with an enjoyment rating by both the husband and the wife. This exercise usually produces a list of ten or fifteen activities that have been rated enjoyable (at least +2) by *both* the husband and the wife. In the weeks to come, I ask them to schedule each of these activities into their recreational time. Some of these choices will be things he may like a bit more than she does, and vice versa, but in every case, they will both be depositing love units as they spend recreational time together. Eventually, they settle on about five activities they both enjoy the most.

No one can do *everything* they would like to do in life. There's just not enough time. So every person must make choices regarding enjoyable activities. Why not select those activities that both you and your spouse enjoy and can do together?

Favorite Recreational Companions

When a couple draws up their master list of mutually enjoyable activities, there are many surprises. The list may contain some activities that neither partner has ever experienced before. The activities simply sounded like they might be enjoyable. Or there may be some activities that the couple didn't realize were mutually enjoyable. They both thought the other disliked doing them.

But there's another surprise that couples often face: they find that something they are already doing together is unpleasant for one of them. What are they to do with that activity?

After Joyce and I were married, she knew what to do with tennis—toss it out of our lives. But there are many wives who would not have made that decision. They would have gone on playing tennis with their husbands, sacrificing their own pleasure so that their husbands could be happy. In other words, deposits into his Love Bank would have created withdrawals in hers.

A husband will often try to do the same thing. He'll do something with his wife that only she enjoys. In those situations, he's not engaged in his favorite recreational activity, and his wife is not his favorite recreational companion. Some other activity is his favorite, and the one who enjoys it with him becomes his favorite recreational companion. If that person is a woman, his marriage is at risk. But even if his companion is a man, his wife is missing a great opportunity to make massive Love Bank deposits.

When I counsel a husband and a wife who have not yet learned how to be each other's favorite recreational companion, I give them a radical assignment:

Engage in only those recreational activities that you and your spouse can enjoy together.

I explain that they can eventually participate in activities apart from each other. But until they become each other's favorite recreational companion, they must spend all their leisure time together.

My assignment is tough because it rules out some activities that a couple may currently be doing together and it also rules out *all* recreational activities that they are doing apart that only one of them enjoys. Despite the difficulty, though, I insist on this rule for spouses who have not yet learned to enjoy recreational activities together.

You can probably imagine the reaction of some. They are appalled that I would even suggest such a thing! It means, for example, that a husband might have to give up *Monday Night Football* if his wife doesn't enjoy watching it with him. Men who thought I was trying to help them out by encouraging their wives to join them in their favorite activities are faced with the prospect of abandoning these activities entirely. I'll admit I've lost the faith of a few spouses on this one. Many have felt I've gone too far.

But once you think it through, you'll likely agree with me, at least on principle. If you were to find recreational activities that both you and your spouse could enjoy together, just as much as you enjoy your favorite activities now, it would definitely improve your feelings for each other. And that's the goal I'm after. What's more important: the quality of your marriage or *Monday Night Football*? In some cases, that's the choice you have.

This assignment of engaging in only mutually appealing activities is not a summons to misery and deprivation, though. For me, it simply means that I should consider Joyce's feelings when selecting a recreational activity from among those I already enjoy. Why should I gain at her expense when we can gain together?

It Just Makes Sense

There are a host of reasons that spouses should discover recreational activities they can enjoy together. For one, doing so reflects the caring love both spouses should have for each other. If one spouse gives up their enjoyment so that the other can be fulfilled, it means that the other is willing to gain at their spouse's expense. That spouse doesn't show care for how the other spouse feels. In my marriage, Joyce and I do not accept sacrifice from each other when it's offered because we care about each other.

A second reason to discover those activities is that they stand up over time. Whatever you and your spouse enjoy together, you are very likely to do again. Do you want more affection? Express affection toward each other in a mutually enjoyable way. Do you want more intimate conversation?

Talk intimately with each other in a mutually enjoyable way. Do you want to make love more often? Make love to each other in a mutually enjoyable way. And when it comes to recreational companionship, if you want to spend more of your leisure time together, make sure that you and your spouse enjoy the type of activity and the way you engage in that activity.

A third reason to discover recreational activities that you can enjoy together is that doing these activities together ensures deposits into each other's Love Bank—especially his. Some of my best feelings occur when I am engaged in a recreational activity. If I share it with Joyce, I associate those good feelings with *her*, which sustains my love for her.

Many spouses, particularly husbands, find my assignment difficult to put into practice. Just the thought of giving up their favorite activities, like hunting or golf, causes depression to set in for some men. I can understand, because men need recreation in their lives to keep going. They use leisure-time activities to recharge themselves. Then some marriage counselor (me) comes along and tells them they can't do the very things that help keep them productive.

Still, I encourage such men to try my plan for just a few months, reminding them that I have not told them to give up recreational pleasures. I have simply advised them to replace old pastimes with some they can share with their wives, or make their wives part of the ones they already enjoy.

In making the changes, a wife should be alert to the possibility that breaking a recreational habit can put her husband into a state of withdrawal. He may miss it terribly at first. She may wonder if she's made a terrible mistake. She didn't mean to force herself on him, although she wants his companionship too. Halfway through their first activity together, she may want to tell him to return to an activity he's left because she feels guilty for taking him away from something she knows he truly enjoys and deserves.

But eventually he will come to enjoy mutually appealing activities even more than those he could not share with his wife. This is because she has an easier time meeting some of his other emotional needs, such as sexual fulfillment, when she is his favorite recreational companion.

If, for one or both of you, an activity fails to be enjoyable after the first time or two, don't give up. Take the time required to gain some skill.

Suppose a wife takes up skiing to please her husband. She needs time to build up the muscles required and to learn the techniques that make her proficient. If he pushes her too fast, she may come to resent it and will quickly turn away from the sport. But if he's patient, she might find it very enjoyable.

However, if the wife tries skiing, gains some proficiency, then still dislikes it, she should have the freedom to tell her husband, "I've tried it. I still don't like it. Let's try something else."

Give yourselves time to adjust and to try new activities. You may have some difficulty accommodating these changes, but you'll find the rewards for your marriage well worth the effort. In my counseling experiences, I've found that couples who limit their recreational activities primarily to those they do together make tremendous gains in compatibility. They also deposit scores of love units into each other's Love Bank.

Recreational Activities and the Time for Undivided Attention

In chapter 2, I encouraged you and your spouse to spend a minimum of fifteen hours a week giving each other undivided attention. During that time, you were to meet each other's intimate emotional needs for affection, intimate conversation, sexual fulfillment, and recreational companionship. I was encouraging you to have fifteen hours of romantic dates each week.

It should not be surprising that women define a romantic experience differently than men. For most women, a romantic evening meets her emotional needs for affection and intimate conversation—maybe an evening of dinner, dancing, and a walk in the moonlight filled with expressions of love and stimulating conversation. Men, on the other hand, can find romance in sexual fulfillment and recreational companionship—watching football on TV with sex during halftime!

Neither perspective on romance in these scenarios works very well for the opposite sex. So prior to marriage, most men and women combine all four needs into a romantic experience. That way, the needs of both men and women are met.

But after marriage, spouses get lazy and want to take shortcuts. Women find time for affection and intimate conversation but might be too busy or too tired for sexual fulfillment or recreational companionship. On the other hand, men can drop almost anything for sexual fulfillment and recreational companionship but can't fit affection or intimate conversation into their busy schedules.

Don't make this mistake in your marriage. You both have intimate emotional needs that should be met by each other. But they're different, and you will be tempted to overlook your spouse's needs. By meeting all four of these needs in a single date, you will have an experience that both of you will consider romantic and you will be making massive Love Bank deposits as well.

With undivided attention in mind, you'll find that some recreational activities cannot be considered part of your fifteen hours. The activities themselves take too much of your attention. That's not to say you shouldn't engage in these activities together. It's just that when considering what to do during your time for undivided attention, make sure that the activity doesn't distract you from each other.

For example, if you focus most of your attention on a movie or a television show, that activity should not be considered part of your time for undivided attention. But if during the show you are expressing affection to each other and your focus of attention is primarily on each other, then it counts. Any recreational activity that allows for affection, intimate conversation, and even sexual fulfillment while you are engaged in the activity is a good candidate.

Dancing, card games, hiking, boating, and even working out at the gym together have been favorites of couples who want a recreational activity that provides an opportunity for undivided attention. But don't include friends or your children with any of those activities. They'll distract you from each other. You should have as much privacy as possible during your fifteen hours.

My assignment to engage in only activities that you and your spouse can enjoy together as recreational companions is not unbearably painful or unrealistic. In fact, it's what you probably did when you first fell in love with each other. It invites both of you to a new level of intimacy and enjoyment of each other. Remember the old adage "The couple that plays together stays together."

QUESTIONS FOR HER

1. Are you your husband's favorite recreational companion? If not, why not?

2. Are you reluctant to encourage your husband to suspend some of his recreational activities until you become his favorite recreational companion? If so, what would help you overcome that reluctance?

3. Does your husband join you in your favorite recreational activities? Are you willing to suspend those activities that he does not find enjoyable so that you can search for mutually enjoyable activities? Do you think he would be willing to do the same?

QUESTIONS FOR HIM

1. Are you your wife's favorite recreational companion? If not, why not?

2. Do you value your leisure time? If so, would having your wife join you make it more relaxing or less relaxing for you? If less relaxing, what could she do to make it more relaxing?

3. Does your wife join you in your favorite recreational activities? Are you willing to suspend those activities that she does not find enjoyable so that you can search for mutually enjoyable activities? Do you think she would be willing to do the same?

TO CONSIDER TOGETHER

1. Use the Recreational Enjoyment Inventory, found in appendix C, to help you discover mutually appealing activities.

2. After identifying activities you both enjoy, schedule time to try each of them. Narrow them down to five or ten that you enjoy the most.

3. Try my "radical assignment": engage in only those recreational activities that you and your spouse can enjoy together until you become each other's favorite recreational companion.

4. In planning your fifteen hours for undivided attention, try to meet all four of the intimate emotional needs each time you have a date: affection, intimate conversation, sexual fulfillment, and recreational companionship. You'll find that each date will require about three or four hours—just as when you were dating each other.

SEVEN

Honesty and Openness

Nicole felt both perplexed and enchanted by Ted's mystique. She had never met a more private man, and he often evaded her questions. Near the end of a date, she might ask him where he was going or what he was planning to do. He would just wink, smile knowingly, and say, "I'll call you tomorrow."

Ted's behavior seemed a bit odd, but Nicole told herself that everybody has a right to privacy. Certainly, Ted had a right to keep *some* things to himself.

Truth be told, Ted had several things he kept to himself—specifically, other girlfriends. When he couldn't conveniently evade Nicole's questions, he took pains to mislead her by telling her about nonexistent projects he had to complete at work. His true projects were dates with other women. Sometimes Nicole suspected he was seeing someone else, but he made such a big thing out of his right to privacy that she felt guilty whenever she questioned his honesty.

Besides, Ted had a lot of what Nicole wanted in a man. He was affectionate and charming. Other women cast envious looks when she walked into a party with such a tall, good-looking man. To ice the cake, he had an excellent income and spent money on her generously. When Ted proposed, all these pluses far outweighed his "I need my privacy" minus.

He'll tell me everything after we're married, Nicole thought.

As it turned out, Ted's behavior did not change after the wedding. In fact, it seemed to become a bigger problem, because now that they lived together, Ted had more occasions than ever to be secretive.

Interestingly enough, all this need for privacy did not mean Ted was seeing another woman. Once he made the marriage commitment, he dropped his other girlfriends to "settle down." But he still reserved the "right" to get home from work when he felt like it. Since his job involved an irregular schedule, Nicole could seldom plan much of anything. Ted would call but would only say, "I'll be late—maybe six thirty. I'm not sure." Nicole learned quickly that she was part of the "keep dinner warm in the oven" brigade. Once he did get home, Ted had none of the charm that had dazzled her during courtship.

He had little to say when it came to making plans. "Can I invite the Morgans for dinner Saturday night?" Nicole would ask.

"Not sure," Ted would reply. "I'll have to see—it's a busy week."

And so it went—from frustration to depression for Nicole. Ted remained faithful, and he really had nothing to hide. For some reason, however, known only to him, he didn't want to share with Nicole what he was doing or thinking.

"At the wedding, our pastor said in marriage two become one," Nicole told her friend Meg. "But Ted and I really can't be one if he won't share his thoughts with me. I've asked if he would go with me to talk with our pastor, but he won't hear of it, and he doesn't want me to go alone. He tells me people at church will find out and misunderstand. I wonder if he's having an affair."

Security and Trust

A sense of security is the bright golden thread woven through most women's five important emotional needs. If a husband does not maintain honest and open communication with his wife, he undermines her trust and eventually destroys her confidence in his care for her.

To feel secure, a wife must trust her husband to give her accurate information about his emotional reactions, his past, his present, and his future. How does he feel? What has he done? What is he thinking or doing right now?

What plans does he have? If she can't trust the signals he sends (or if, as in the case of Ted, he refuses to send any signals), she has no foundation on which to build a solid relationship. Instead of adjusting to him, she always feels off balance; instead of growing *with* him, she grows *away* from him.

The wife who can't trust her husband to give her the information she needs also lacks a means of negotiating with him. Negotiation between a husband and a wife is an essential building block in the success of any marriage, but without honesty and openness, a couple can resolve or decide very little.

Withholding information in marriage is bad enough. But when a spouse provides misleading or downright false information, it's a disaster. I cover the topic of dishonesty in chapter 6 of my book *Love Busters* because it's one of the six most destructive habits a spouse can have in marriage. However, in this chapter, I will focus attention on only Ted's problem. He's not necessarily being dishonest—he's simply keeping his thoughts, activities, and plans to himself. He's failing to meet Nicole's need for honesty and openness.

Being Open

I tell couples I counsel that transparency is one of the most important qualities in a successful marriage. Nothing should be hidden from each other. Your spouse should know you better than anyone else. But sadly, within a few short counseling sessions, I often know more about each spouse than they do about each other. I'm not clairvoyant or particularly sensitive to understanding people, but when I ask them questions, they both give me honest answers. They know they need help, and they also know that the more information they provide, the more helpful I will be to them.

As each spouse "comes clean" with me, I get a clearer picture of both of them than they have ever had of each other. For years, they have wandered around blindly in the smoke screens each has laid down for the other. When they talk to me, they have no need for a smoke screen, and the real problem or issue starts to emerge.

In most cases I've witnessed, it isn't the wife who does most of the hiding—it's the husband. She's the one who usually asks him "What are you thinking?" and "How are you feeling?" and "What are you planning?"

Nicole asked Ted these questions many times, without getting any satisfactory responses. In fact, he usually made a joke of it. "Are you a reporter? Are you writing a book?" he would ask disrespectfully.

The result was that Nicole's emotional need for honesty and openness was unmet. But almost equally important, she wasn't able to grow in her understanding of Ted. After five years of marriage, she hardly knew him.

Privacy

Many people ask me, "When you say I have to be honest and open with my spouse, aren't you taking away all my privacy?" If by *privacy* this person means keeping part of himself or herself hidden, I hold firmly to my conviction that this word has no place in a marriage relationship. I have seen too many marital disasters follow the compromise of my principle. Although you may find it threatening to think your spouse might have the right to read your email or go through your text messages, I believe this kind of openness is indispensable for a healthy marriage.

When I "protect my privacy," it makes me less transparent to my wife. Joyce is the one person who needs to know me best, and I need to provide her with all the information—including the warts. Not only should I answer her questions truthfully, but I should also avoid "lies of silence" and readily volunteer information as well. In other words, I must share myself with her in every way possible.

Essential Ingredients

There are three very important reasons why honesty and openness are absolutely essential in marriage. First, they provide a clear road map for marital adjustment. A husband and a wife who are honest and open with each other can identify their problems very quickly and, if they know how to negotiate, dispose of them very swiftly. A lack of transparency covers up both the problems themselves and the solutions to those problems. The more facts you and your spouse have, the better you'll understand each other. And the more you understand each other, the more likely it is that you'll come up with resolutions to your conflicts.

The second reason honesty and openness are essential in marriage is that dishonesty, or covering the truth in some way, is painfully offensive. That offense causes such massive Love Bank withdrawals that I include it as one of the six major Love Busters. As I mentioned earlier in this chapter, I discuss dishonesty and how to overcome it in my book *Love Busters*.

But the third reason that honesty and openness are essential in marriage is the topic of this chapter—they meet an important emotional need. For many, especially women, honesty and openness deposit so many love units that a woman can fall in love with someone simply because he has been radically honest with her. She needs a clear and unobstructed view into the mind of the one with whom she will share herself.

The need for honesty and openness in marriage is so important to most women that I've given couples a rule that explains how far a husband (and a wife) should go in revealing himself (and herself). I call it the Policy of Radical Honesty.

> **Reveal to your spouse as much information about yourself as you know—your thoughts, feelings, habits, likes, dislikes, history, daily activities, and future plans.**

To make this clearer to you and easier to understand, I'll break the policy down into four parts.

1. *Emotional honesty*. Reveal your thoughts, feelings, likes, and dislikes. In other words, reveal your emotional reactions—both positive and negative—to the events of your life, particularly to your spouse's behavior.

2. *Historical honesty*. Reveal information about your personal history, particularly events that demonstrate personal weakness or failure.

3. *Current honesty*. Reveal information about the events of your day. Provide your spouse with a calendar of your activities, with special emphasis on those that may affect them.

4. *Future honesty*. Reveal your thoughts and plans regarding future activities and objectives.

Let's take a careful look at each of the four parts of the Policy of Radical Honesty.

Emotional Honesty

Most spouses do their best to make each other happy. But their efforts, however sincere, are often misdirected. They aim at the wrong target.

Imagine a man who buys his wife flowers every night on the way home from work. What a wonderful thing to do—except that his wife is allergic to them. Because she appreciates the gesture, though, she never mentions her allergies but just sniffles in silence. Soon, however, she begins to dread the thought of her husband coming home with those terrible flowers. Meanwhile, he's getting bored with the marriage because she is always feeling lousy and never has energy to do anything. But, of course, he won't ask her what is at the root of those things for her nor tell her how he feels.

This couple's marriage is in trouble, not because of any lack of effort but because of their ignorance—ignorance caused by a lack of honesty. He thinks he's doing a good thing by bringing home flowers, but he doesn't realize that the flowers are the cause of his wife's malaise. Let's say that in his effort to show even more love for her, he brings home more and more flowers. Ultimately, she collapses on the couch, gasping for breath, surrounded by flowers, while he wonders what went wrong.

Of course, this is a preposterous story, but it portrays the way many spouses misfire in their attempts to please each other. Their lack of honesty and openness keeps them from correcting their real problems.

Some people, like Ted in the opening scenario, find it difficult to express their emotional reactions, particularly the negative ones. But negative feelings serve a valuable purpose in a marriage. They are a signal that something is wrong. If you successfully steer clear of the enemies of intimate conversation—demands, disrespect, and anger—your expression of negative feelings can alert both you and your spouse to an adjustment that must be made.

Let me make that last point once more for emphasis: if you can express your reactions without being demanding, without expressing disrespect, and without becoming angry, your reactions will become an essential ingredient in helping you understand each other. On the other hand, if you express your reactions in the form of demands, disrespect, or anger, the message you will be sending will not create understanding. Instead, it will communicate an unwillingness to understand.

Honesty and openness enable spouses to make appropriate adjustments to each other. And adjustment is what a good marriage is all about. The circumstances that led you into your blissful union will certainly change, if they haven't already, and you need to learn to roll with the tide. Both of you are growing and changing with each new day, and you must constantly adjust to each other's changes. But how can you know how to adjust if you're not receiving accurate information about these changes? You're flying blind, like a pilot whose instrument panel has shorted out.

> **Emotional Honesty:**
> Reveal your emotional reactions—both positive and negative—to the events of your life, particularly to your spouse's behavior.

You need accurate data from each other. Without it, unhappy situations can go on and on—like the flowers piling up in the allergic woman's home.

But the expression of your deepest feelings does more than help you make correct adjustments to each other. It makes Love Bank deposits. Nicole *needed* Ted to express his feelings to her. It would have helped her become emotionally bonded to him—two becoming one. His failure to express his deepest thoughts and feelings made her feel locked out of his life.

Historical Honesty

Should your skeletons stay in the closet? Some say yes. Lock the door, hide the key, leave well enough alone. Communicate your past misdeeds only on a need-to-know basis.

But your spouse has a right to know, and needs to know, all about your past. Whatever embarrassing experiences or serious mistakes are in your past, you should come clean with your spouse in the present.

Your personal history holds significant information about you—information about your strengths and weaknesses. If your spouse is to make appropriate adjustments, they should understand both your good and your bad experiences so they know when you can be relied upon and when you might need help.

No area of your life should be kept secret. All your spouse's questions should be answered fully and completely. Periods of poor adjustment in your past should be given special attention because problems of the past are commonly problems of the future. A man who has had an affair in the past is particularly vulnerable to another one. If a woman has been chemically dependent in the past, she'll be susceptible to drug or alcohol abuse in the future. If you express your past mistakes openly, your spouse can understand your weaknesses, and together you can avoid conditions that tend to create the same problems for you.

Not only should you explain your past to your spouse, but you should also encourage your spouse to gather information about you from those who knew you before you met. Talk with several significant people from each other's past. It can be a very helpful eye-opener!

> **Historical Honesty:** Reveal information about your personal history, particularly events that demonstrate personal weakness or failure.

I also encourage you to reveal to each other all romantic relationships you've had in the past. Names should be included along with a description of what happened to end the relationship.

"But if I tell my wife what I've done, she'll never trust me again."

"If my husband finds out about my past, he'll be crushed. It will ruin his whole image of me."

I have heard these protests from various clients trying to hide their past. "Why dig it all up?" they ask. "Let that old affair stay buried in ancient history. Why not just leave that little demon alone?" I answer that it's not a little demon but an extremely important part of their personal story that says something about their habits and character.

But what if you haven't strayed since it happened? What if you've seen a pastor or other counselor regularly to hold you accountable? Why put your spouse through the agony of a revelation that could ruin your relationship forever?

If that's your argument, I'd say you don't give your spouse much credit. Honesty and openness don't drive a spouse away—*dishonesty* does. When you hold something back, your spouse tries to guess what it is. If they are correct, then you must continually lie to cover your tracks. If they are incorrect, they develop a false understanding of you and your predispositions.

Maybe you don't really want to be known for who you are. That's sad, isn't it? You'd rather keep your secret than experience one of life's greatest joys—to be loved and accepted in spite of known weaknesses.

While revealing your past will strengthen your marriage, it's not necessarily painless. Some spouses have difficulty adjusting to revelations that have been kept secret for years—the saint they thought they married turns out to be a mere mortal. To control the emotional damage of particularly shocking revelations, it may be helpful to express them to your spouse in the presence of a professional counselor. Some people may need some personal support to help them adjust to the reality of their spouse's past.

In cases I've witnessed, however, spouses tend to react more negatively to the long-term deception than to the concealed event. The thoughtless act might be accepted and forgiven, but the cover-up is often harder to understand. If you reveal something before your spouse discovers it, though, it's proof that you are taking honesty in your marriage seriously.

You may find the idea of revealing your past frightening, and that's understandable. But let me assure you that I've never seen a marriage destroyed by truth. When truth is revealed, there may be negative reactions and some shaky times, but ultimately the truth makes marriages stronger. On the other hand, hiding the truth destroys intimacy, romantic love, and marriages.

Current Honesty

In good marriages, spouses become so interdependent that sharing a daily schedule is essential to their coordination of activities. In weak marriages, spouses are reluctant to reveal their schedules because they often engage in activities that they want to keep from each other. So they hide the details of their day, telling themselves, *What he doesn't know won't hurt him* or *She's happier not knowing everything.*

But let's think back to Ted and Nicole for a moment. Ted's activities were innocent. He wasn't doing anything that would have been alarming to

Nicole. By keeping them secret, however, Ted left Nicole's imagination to run wild. She even suspected that he might be having an affair. His failure to meet her emotional need for honesty and openness prevented him from making Love Bank deposits. But her suspicions that he might be having an affair made huge Love Bank withdrawals. He could have made deposits and avoided withdrawals if he'd simply shown her his daily schedule.

Make it easy for your spouse to find you in an emergency or to contact you during the day just to say hello. Keep your cell phones close by so that you can call each other 24/7.

> **Current History:** Reveal information about the events of your day. Provide your spouse with a calendar of your activities, with special emphasis on those that may affect them.

Current honesty protects your spouse from potentially damaging predispositions and inappropriate activities. When you know that you'll be telling your spouse what you've been up to, you'll be far less likely to have what I call a *secret second life*. The easiest way to stay out of trouble is to shine a bright light on everything you do. Honesty and openness are that bright light.

Future Honesty

After I've made such a big issue of revealing past indiscretions, you can imagine how I feel about revealing future plans. They're *much* easier to discuss with your spouse, yet many spouses make plans independently of each other. Why?

Some people believe that communicating future plans just gives a spouse the opportunity to quash them. They have their sights set on a certain goal, and they don't want anything to stand in their way. But that's shortsighted thinking. If you keep your plans a secret, you may succeed in avoiding trouble in the present, but eventually the future will arrive and your plans will be revealed. And at that point, your spouse will be hurt in two ways. First, because you didn't consider their feelings when you made your plans, and second, because you didn't tell them your plans. Love Bank withdrawals are certain to be made. So don't overlook this component of an honest and open relationship.

In chapter 2, I encouraged spouses to make time every week, say at 3:30 Sunday afternoon, to schedule fifteen hours of undivided attention for the coming week. If you don't schedule time for undivided attention, it won't happen, and you won't meet each other's most important emotional needs. But another purpose of this time is to review each other's entire schedule for the week. Each of you should know what the other is planning to do because almost everything you do will affect each other. You will be making either Love Bank deposits or Love Bank withdrawals with what you plan to do.

> **Future History:** Reveal your thoughts and plans regarding future activities and objectives.

Are You Encouraging or Discouraging Honesty and Openness?

In this chapter, I have primarily focused attention on husbands and their unwillingness to be open and honest. But now I'd like to turn to wives. Do you do anything to discourage your husband in this area? More specifically, do your values encourage or discourage your husband to be open and honest with you? Do your reactions encourage or discourage your husband to reveal the truth, even when it's unpleasant to hear? To see how you rate, answer these questions:

1. If the truth is terribly upsetting to you, do you want your spouse to be honest and open *only* at a time when you are emotionally prepared?
2. Do you keep some aspects of your life secret, and do you encourage your spouse to respect *your* privacy in those areas?
3. Do you like to create a certain mystery between you and your spouse?
4. Are there subjects or situations about which you want to avoid radical honesty?
5. Do you ever make selfish demands when your spouse is open and honest with you?
6. Do you ever make disrespectful judgments when your spouse is open and honest with you?

7. Do you ever have angry outbursts when your spouse is open and honest with you?
8. Do you dwell on mistakes when your spouse is open and honest with you?

If you answered yes to any of the first four questions, you tend to compromise on the value of honesty and openness. You might feel that your marriage is better off with less information in certain situations. That little crack is all some husbands need to keep their distance emotionally. You see, there are always "reasons" to be less than radically honest. And as soon as you allow one reason to sneak in, it will invite all its friends in too.

If you answered yes to questions 5, 6, 7, or 8, you are punishing honesty and openness. The way to help your spouse learn to be transparent is to minimize the negative consequences of his truthful revelations. If your spouse is faced with a fight whenever truth is revealed, he'll keep his thoughts to himself. But what if there are no demands, no judgments, no anger, no dwelling on mistakes? If you can eliminate these enemies of intimate conversation, you'll make it much easier for your spouse to be honest and open with you.

How Mutual Honesty Can Rescue a Marriage

What happens when a marriage so lacks honesty and openness that it leads to the ultimate dishonesty of an affair? Can coming clean with your spouse help, or will it spell sure death for the relationship?

In a common scenario, I sit down to counsel with a husband who tells me, right up front, that he has been involved in an extramarital affair. He has not told his wife about it, yet he feels "terribly guilty."

As counseling proceeds, I suggest that he confess this to his wife. With some fear and trepidation, he does so, and she responds with predictable reactions: anger, anxiety, and finally depression. But with my guidance, he does something that gives her hope for the future. He commits himself to taking extraordinary precautions to avoid any contact with the other woman and to become radically honest with her in the future. He also agrees to follow a program of recovery that I have recommended. She begins to see how their marriage might survive if he keeps those commitments. It can then be rebuilt on mutual honesty for the first time.

When spouses deal with trying to survive an affair, I train them to become thoroughly candid with each other. They must conceal nothing of what they think or feel. Only through total openness can an honest relationship emerge. If they compromise at any point, it will only undermine the rebuilding process.

You may wonder if it is always wise for the unfaithful spouse to confess their sins to the other. In my experience, such a confession has never been the primary cause of a divorce. Some couples do divorce because of an affair, but not because they have spoken honestly with each other. Instead, it's quite common for the betrayed spouse—husband or wife—to emerge from the initial shock of learning about the affair willing to examine and consider ways to resolve the marriage's problems. But the unfaithful spouse is unwilling to follow a plan of recovery that gives the betrayed spouse hope for their future together.

In chapter 14 of this book, "How to Survive an Affair," I explain how to turn this willingness of the betrayed spouse to give the marriage a chance into complete marital recovery. In the end, trust is restored because the unfaithful spouse learns how to be honest and open and, over time, proves his trustworthiness.

A spouse with a history of secrecy may insist that their confession of the affair by itself proves they have reformed. They may want their spouse to begin to trust them again immediately. But that won't happen. You cannot turn on trust like a light switch. Rather, it takes numerous experiences of honesty and openness along with caring behavior to demonstrate change.

As I mentioned earlier, I recommend strongly that spouses provide each other with a daily schedule, which can be easily checked for accuracy. They should be able to locate and contact each other by cell phone. If the schedule changes during the day, they should notify each other immediately. If trust must be restored, they should be able to verify their presence at places on their schedule in a way that avoids any embarrassment.

Spouses who have no reason to mistrust each other don't check up on each other throughout the day. They're satisfied that their word is enough. But when there is a reason, such as a past affair, their willingness to let each other investigate their whereabouts to prove their honesty is necessary to restore trust. Expecting a betrayed spouse to trust an unfaithful spouse without proof is completely unreasonable. It's the proof of honesty and openness that restores trust.

Before we move on to the next chapter, I must make one other very important point regarding trust. While honesty and openness are essential in building trust, our behavior must also be trustworthy. Everything you decide to do must protect the feelings and interests of your spouse if you are to be trusted. If you tell your spouse everything you do each day yet do what you please with no regard for the effect it has on them, how do you expect your spouse to trust you? It's only when you are honest and open and also are making every decision with your spouse's interests in mind that you build a strong foundation for trust. I develop this important concept more fully in the opening chapters of *Love Busters*.

A woman *needs* to trust her husband. And her husband's openness and honesty with her go a long way to enable her to do that. Whatever advantage a man may gain in being secretive, closed, or even dishonest, he gains at the expense of his wife's security and marital fulfillment. She must come to find him predictable; a blending of her mind with his should exist so that she can "read his mind." When a husband becomes that transparent, she is fulfilled—the two become one.

QUESTIONS FOR HIM

1. Are any of the parts of my Policy of Radical Honesty difficult for you—emotional honesty, historical honesty, current honesty, or future honesty? If so, which ones, and why are they difficult?

2. Do you agree with the contention that there should be no privacy in your marriage—that is, neither one of you should keep facts regarding yourself from the other? Why or why not?

3. Does your wife encourage or discourage honesty and openness? Does she do this with her values and/or her reaction to your honesty?

QUESTIONS FOR HER

1. In your personal hierarchy of needs, how essential are your husband's honesty and openness? Do you agree that honesty and openness are one of your five most important emotional needs in marriage? Why or why not?

2. Has your husband made it difficult for you to understand him? Has he kept his thoughts and feelings, personal history, current activities, or plans for the future from you? If so, how does this make you feel?

3. In what ways do you wish your husband were more open and honest with you? Do you wish for more emotional honesty, historical honesty, current honesty, and/or future honesty?

TO CONSIDER TOGETHER

1. Discuss your answers to the above questions. They will be a good test of how open and honest your marriage really is.

2. From the "Questionnaires" section of the Marriage Builders website (www.marriagebuilders.com), print two copies of the Personal History Questionnaire, one for each of you. After you have completed the forms, read each other's answers and discuss them. Freely ask questions that are triggered by any of the answers you read.

3. If either of you needs help overcoming dishonesty, read together chapter 6, "Dishonesty," in *Love Busters*. It will offer you a plan to help rid your marriage of this very destructive habit.

EIGHT

Physical Attractiveness

When Brittany and Josh started dating, he thought she was a real knockout. Her figure, makeup, hairstyle, and choice of clothes all came together to create just about everything he'd ever wanted physically in a woman. About eight months later, when Josh proposed, she said yes.

When I counseled Brittany and Josh about five years later, I started by talking with them separately. Josh told me, "The first thing she did after we got married was quit her job. Then she stayed home, eating all day. She's gained about one hundred pounds since we've been married."

"Have you said anything about her weight?" I asked.

"Yes, many times. In fact, it's a sore point between us. But she just says, 'I want you to love me for who I am. If you'd love me and accept me unconditionally, then I could easily lose the weight.' But the less I say, the more weight she gains," Josh continued.

Next I talked to Brittany to get her side. She confessed to me that though she had been in the best shape of her life when they had met, she had always struggled with her weight and self-image. She also admitted that she had never talked to Josh much about that. So when he expressed concern with her weight gain, she felt terribly hurt.

Granted, some men do not care about the physical appearance of their wives. They can be overweight or underweight; it makes no difference. They have other emotional needs that are far more important than the need for physical attractiveness. But Brittany had not married one of these men. In fact, she had married a man for whom physical attractiveness was near the very top of his list.

Some women also have a strong need for an attractive husband. Two other spouses I counseled, Beth and Cory, were both track stars when they attended college together. She was very attracted to him physically, and when they married, she envisioned the two of them continuing to exercise regularly to stay in shape. But he didn't do that after they were married. Instead, he gave up all forms of exercise and became a couch potato, no longer caring about his appearance at all.

Many men think that the emotional needs of women are trivial needs. Many women think that the emotional needs of men are trivial. But they are not trivial to those who have them. Brittany felt that physical attractiveness was trivial because she didn't have that need. So she concluded that Josh's shallow sense of values was the culprit. If he would grow up and be more mature, he would look beyond her appearance.

Why All the Fuss about Looking Good?

People often challenge me when I list physical attractiveness as one of the most important emotional needs of most men. In fact, some have written me saying that when they came to this chapter, they lost all confidence in my judgment. Shouldn't we be looking beyond the surface and into more meaningful human characteristics, such as honesty, trustworthiness, and caring?

As I mentioned earlier, not all men have an emotional need for physical attractiveness. They marry women who meet other emotional needs. But in Josh's case, one of the many reasons he fell in love with Brittany was because she met this need so effectively while they were dating. Brittany also quit her job after they married. But Josh never complained about that change because he didn't have a need that I'll introduce in the next chapter—the need for financial support. He was happy to support her financially, one of her emotional needs, and hoped she'd continue to meet all his emotional needs in return.

So she enrolled in an exercise program, began eating healthier, and lost forty pounds in three months as a result. Josh even joined her in the exercise program. A year later she was healthier than ever, and both of them enjoyed the extra time they had together.

Brittany's work toward a heathier lifestyle was not only a gesture of caring love for Josh but also a very effective way to care for herself. It greatly improved her health and self-esteem.

Look Good to Feel Good

A man with a need for an attractive spouse feels good whenever he looks at his attractive wife. In fact, that is what emotional needs are all about. When a spouse's emotional needs are met, they feel fulfilled, and when they're not met, they feel frustrated.

Many women rank this need among their most important emotional needs as well. But I've found that most women are far more likely to fall in love with men who meet other emotional needs, such as affection, intimate conversation, honesty and openness, financial support, and family commitment. Physical attractiveness is much farther down their list.

I remember counseling an overweight, balding man who was twenty years older than his very pretty wife. Nonetheless, she was crazy about him, and they shared a very active sex life. What did she see in him? That's just the point. She saw a warm and sensitive man who was kind and generous and who cared for her as deeply as she cared for him.

She simply had different emotional needs. Physical attractiveness did not do as much for her as it did for him.

How to Improve Your Physical Appearance

Any husband or wife can enhance their attractiveness to each other. There are plenty of books, videos, diet programs, and other products designed to help people shape up, dress with style, color their hair properly, and so forth. When I counsel those who want to improve their physical appearance, I focus attention on five major areas that are particularly important in staying or becoming attractive. Let's give them a quick review.

Weight and Fitness

Almost all the complaints I've heard regarding a spouse's physical attractiveness fall into the category of being overweight and physically unfit. Technically, these are two different categories because a person can be overweight yet physically fit and healthy, or they can be a "healthy" weight yet physically unfit. But the complaints that I hear tend to combine them into a single issue: the complaining spouse wants their spouse to possess their definition of physical fitness.

A host of diet and exercise programs have flooded the market, so I won't try to repeat what has already been proven to be effective. But I will suggest some of the simplest ways to maintain a healthy weight and to keep physically fit.

As part of your fifteen hours of undivided attention, exercise together. Whether it's biking or going to a fitness center, do it together and make it a part of your romantic dates. I've found that one of the best ways to make massive Love Bank deposits is to be together when you go through a workout routine. In one case, exercising together was all it took for a couple I was counseling to restore their love for each other.

When you shop for food, try to keep processed food loaded with sugar and simple carbohydrates at a minimum. Your children may complain, but they'll be as healthy as you will become by avoiding those foods.

Makeup

When Joyce and I operated a dating service, Joyce would often help women with the way they applied makeup. If makeup is something a woman enjoys wearing and something her spouse enjoys on her, she may benefit from learning more application techniques. When the single women Joyce helped made some changes, single men almost always paid more attention. A husband might also appreciate his wife's efforts to improve her use of makeup, especially if makeup is something he likes seeing on her. While your objective is to meet your husband's need for physical attractiveness, *you* should also like the change. Don't ever use cosmetics in a way that makes you feel uncomfortable.

Hairstyle

Hairstyles, like everything else, can create deposits or withdrawals in a spouse's Love Bank. If a husband or a wife understands their spouse's need for physical attractiveness, they will work with them to meet this need. In my experience, chances are great that a wife will find that her husband has fairly good taste.

I've encouraged husbands and wives who want to see a hairstyle change in their spouse to go to the internet to see literally hundreds of popular options for men and women of all ages. When you see something that both of you might like, take a copy to your barber or hairdresser and have them try to duplicate it. If the result is mutually acceptable, you have a new, more attractive hairstyle. But if it doesn't turn out as expected, keep looking.

When Joyce and I first moved to Minnesota fifty years ago, I decided to grow a mustache for the first time. She agreed. But when I wanted to cut it off later, she objected. I still have that mustache that Joyce found so attractive. Why would I even think of changing an aspect of my appearance that works well for her? And I'm okay with having had a mustache for the past fifty years.

Clothes

As with cosmetics and hairstyle, the same principle applies to clothing: dress to be attractive to your spouse *and* comfortable with your own look.

Joyce and I shop for each other's clothes together. Neither of us wears anything that the other one finds objectionable. We do that to be as attractive as possible to each other. I highly recommend this approach to the purchase of clothing.

Personal Hygiene

To be honest, I've hardly ever counseled a woman who needed help with her personal hygiene, but I've helped many men with this problem.

Kent was a very successful farmer. He was a decent man, but having been single for the better part of his adult life, he had paid little attention to his appearance. Jessica thought she could overlook his outward appearance and love him for his inner qualities. After they were married, however, she found that his appearance turned her off completely.

When they came for their first appointment, Kent complained that Jessica refused to make love to him. She came up with every excuse, and he finally thought a counselor might help.

"I just can't have sex with him," she explained. "When I married him, I thought he would be more appealing to me, but it's getting worse. He'll probably divorce me, but I just can't do it."

When Kent came into the office, his body odor just about knocked me over! He had been chewing tobacco, and his teeth were caked with residue. His hair was a mess, and his clothes looked like he'd slept in them. I had counseled many men who had trouble keeping themselves clean, but Kent was beyond anything I could have imagined.

"She doesn't like sex" was his explanation for their problem.

I had a different theory. "I think I can help you," I replied, "but you'll have to do everything I recommend. Within a few weeks, I think your problem will be solved."

I gave him this assignment:

1. Take a shower every morning and evening due to the nature of your work.
2. With Jessica's help, buy a new wardrobe. Let her pick out clothes for you to wear each day. Never wear anything you've worn the day before unless it has been washed.
3. Go to a dentist and have your teeth cleaned. Stop chewing tobacco.
4. Comb your hair and shave every morning before breakfast.

Fulfilling this assignment was quite a commitment for Kent. He was used to going weeks without a shower. He wore the same pants and shirt day after day, and he hadn't been to a dentist since he was a teenager. But he agreed to it, believing me when I said it would help his sexual relationship with Jessica.

Then I gave Jessica her assignment. Shop with Kent for clothes, pick out something for him to wear every day, and see to it that the clothes are clean. I also asked her if she would be willing to consider making love to him every day for one week after he followed through on all his assignments.

A deal was struck, and Kent was off to the dentist and clothing store. He kept his part of the bargain, and Jessica kept hers. After he had clean teeth, clean clothes, and a clean body, Jessica made love to him once a day for a week.

At their next appointment, I could hardly recognize Kent. What a transformation! And they were holding hands in the waiting room.

I'm sure they didn't make love every day from then on, but they were both satisfied with their new sexual compatibility. Kent had learned a very important lesson about Jessica. His physical appearance, especially his smell, was important to her sexually.

The hygiene problems of most men are not as extreme as Kent's, but lesser problems can still have a devastating effect on wives, especially while making love. A woman wants to be physically close to the man she loves, especially if he looks and smells good.

The Value of Making the Most of What You Have

Consider what it means to be physically attractive. It simply means that your appearance makes your spouse feel good. You meet an emotional need by the way you look. It's a way of demonstrating caring love for your spouse.

People can be attractive in many ways. Those with an attractive personality are usually meeting the emotional need of intimate conversation. In fact, whenever someone meets any of our emotional needs, we usually consider that person attractive. So if your physical attractiveness can meet an emotional need of your spouse, why ignore it? Why not make Love Bank deposits whenever you have a chance?

The changes in appearance I've witnessed in my clients not only have met spouses' needs but also have made my clients feel much better about themselves. The changes have made them more successful in business and have improved their health. It's one of those efforts that pays dividends in ways that go far beyond the marriage itself.

QUESTIONS FOR HER

1. Is physical attractiveness one of your top five emotional needs in your marriage? If so, are you willing to lovingly share with your husband what you find the most attractive about him and for him to tell you the same in return?
2. Are you honest, and kind, with your husband about your feelings regarding this emotional need?
3. How much care do you take in the way you look?

QUESTIONS FOR HIM

1. Is physical attractiveness one of your top five emotional needs in your marriage? If so, are you willing to lovingly share with your wife what you find the most attractive about her and for her to tell you the same in return?
2. Are you honest, and kind, with your wife about your feelings regarding this emotional need?
3. How much care do you take in the way you look?

TO CONSIDER TOGETHER

1. Sit down with your collection of photographs—especially those from the days when you were dating and from your wedding day. Compare the way you looked then with the way you look today. How do you feel as you reflect on those days?
2. Share your answers to the above questions with each other. Be respectful but honest.
3. How can you kindly share with each other what physical attraction means to you?

NINE

Financial Support

Taylor had been raised in an upper-middle class American home. She attended the state university, where she majored in art, history—and Jon. They married while still in school.

Jon finished his undergraduate work and also earned a master's degree in fine arts. But once he was out of school, he could find no work that utilized his training. He tried to move into the world of commercial art, but the competition was fierce. Two years after graduation, he still had not found full-time work. He kept very busy with his painting and drawing, but his income was poor and unpredictable. During the first six years of their marriage, his jobs or assignments never lasted longer than six months.

Consequently, Taylor found herself working full-time as a receptionist to help make ends meet. She wanted to have children, but their finances prevented it. They lived in a modest apartment. Little money was available for extras, and they could afford only one inexpensive car.

During a conversation with Ann, a coworker, she said, "I feel so bad for Jon. He's so good at what he does, but it's hard for an artist to find a steady job." Then she broke down and started crying.

"Taylor!" Ann's voice conveyed more compassion than alarm.

"I don't think Jon will ever earn much," Taylor sobbed. "We'll never have anything."

"It's probably none of my business, but Jon has a good thing going," Ann suggested. "He can spend all day enjoying art while you're here supporting him. If he hadn't married you, he'd be working like the rest of us. I don't think he's being fair to you."

That started Taylor thinking. *Jon is using me!* she thought. *He's doing what he enjoys at my expense. If he cared about me, he'd give up his artwork for a profession that could support us.* She became increasingly resentful about how trapped she was.

Do Women Marry Men for Their Financial Support?

Over the past fifty years, I've witnessed a revolution in the workforce. When I started my career as a psychologist, men dominated the field. My class of twenty-five PhD candidates included only two women. Today women dominate psychology. But the revolution has affected not only my profession. Overall, women now outnumber men in most careers; they are in the working majority.

So you might think that the cultural shift toward women in the workplace would change a woman's need for financial support. That's not necessarily the case.

As a test of whether women still marry for money, I will sometimes ask an audience of young couples a question. "If just before your wedding your spouse had announced that you should not expect him or her to earn much of an income, would you have tied the knot? Raise your hand if you would have gone through with the wedding knowing that you alone would have to support your spouse financially." While almost all the men raise their hands, hardly a single woman's hand joins them.

In truth, most women *do* marry a man expecting his partnership in financial support. They want their husbands to partner with them in supporting their family together and managing their finances together. Most men do not have that same need.

Resentment for *Having* to Work

Most wives expect their husbands not only to be employed but also to earn enough to support their family. Time after time, many married women have told me that they resent *having* to work, particularly after having their first child. The women I talk to usually want a *choice* between following a career and being a homemaker—or possibly they want a combination of the two. Often, they want to be homemakers in their younger years, while their children are small. Later, after the children are older, they want to develop their careers.

However, hard reality for many women today dictates that they must work to help make ends meet, even when their children are small. Their husbands simply can't handle the basic monthly bills on their own.

Please understand that I'm not against women who want careers, and I don't oppose women who choose a career early in life. My daughter earned a PhD and is a licensed psychologist. She raised her two daughters while employed. I am proud of her achievement, and she is happy with her dual role as homemaker and psychologist. And so is her husband.

I wish, rather, to stress the principle that many women need to have the *choice* of whether or not to work once they have children. If they *do* choose a career and begin pursuing it, they should still have the choice of leaving their career for a period of time to raise their children. The easiest way for that choice to be available to them is to not spend the money they earn on basic support of the family. What the wife earns should either be invested, saved, or spent on extras that the family can live without. To put it all very simply, I feel that when a wife has financial support as one of her most important emotional needs, a family should learn how to live on what a husband can earn in a normal workweek.

I realize that what I say will not be popular with many couples. Many will simply write me off as unrealistic. Don't I know that today a couple simply cannot live on one salary? No, I really don't know that, as I will explain later in this chapter. In fact, I know that a family *can* live on one salary, and I will show you how it can be done. I simply want to emphasize that there are many women whose need for financial support is deep and should be treated seriously. Most men don't have this need. If a husband's salary pays the bills, he will probably feel quite content if his wife who is home with his children earns little or nothing. By contrast, I have met very few women who sincerely feel content with a husband who earns little or nothing.

If a husband identifies financial support as one of his top emotional needs, his reasons for doing so are usually very different than her reasons. His reasons are typically due to needing assistance in carrying the load of providing for the family. He finds it helpful in sharing the responsibility of making ends meet.

But men rarely want to have the option of working full-time or becoming a full-time homemaker, as many wives want. That difference is due to the difference in how powerful this emotional need is for many women.

The Necessary Good—a Budget

Every family must come to grips with what it can afford. Some couples look at budgets as a "necessary evil." I like to call a budget a "necessary good," and I recommend it to almost every couple I counsel. I have yet to meet a couple who at times didn't want to buy more than they could afford.

A budget helps you discover what a certain quality of life really costs. To help you more fully understand the quality of life you can afford, I recommend three budgets: one to describe what you *need*, one to describe what you *want*, and one to describe what you can *afford*.

The *needs budget* should include the monthly cost of meeting the necessities of your life, items you would be uncomfortable, or even unhealthy, without.

The *wants budget* includes the cost of meeting all your needs and wants—things that bring special pleasure to your life. It should be realistic, however.

The *affordable budget* begins with your income and should first include the cost of the needs budget. If there is money left over when the cost of meeting all your needs is covered, your most important wants are then included in this budget until your expenses match your income.

To put these budgets in the context of a woman's need for financial support, I recommend that only the husband's income be used in the needs budget. In other words, if his income is sufficient to meet all the needs of the family, by definition he has met his wife's need for financial support. Without these budgets, his success in meeting this need may not be obvious to her.

Both spouses' incomes are included in the wants budget. If her income, when added to his, covers all their needs and wants, they must go no further. But if the cost of their needs and wants is more than their joint income, the affordable budget strips away their lowest priority wants, leaving them with needs covered by his income and wants they can afford covered by her income. These three budgets make it clear that the wife's income is helping the family improve its quality of life, providing for wants that are beyond their basic needs.

Some women want to work for the challenges and rewards of a career; for others, it's to have a break from the children. But regardless of the reason, if her husband's income supports the family's basic needs, she's not working to support herself or her family. She may decide that she'll have a higher quality of life by *not* working as much. She may not have as much money, but she has more time with her family.

I've been amazed by the number of women who feel much better toward their husband when they realize that his income actually pays for her needs and those of the children. The Financial Support Inventory, found in appendix D, will help you create a needs budget, a wants budget, and an affordable budget.

Can He Earn More?

But what happens when a husband's income is not sufficient to pay for the needs budget expenses and the wife has financial support as an important emotional need? Doing without their basic needs is an unacceptable option for many women. Resentful as they might be about working, they may prefer working over having an impoverished way of life.

I've met countless couples caught in this trap. The husband works as hard as he can, coming home tired every night, but his paycheck just won't go far enough. His wife faces the impossible choice of being unhappy while working to make up the difference or being unhappy while putting up with what seems to her an intolerably poor quality of life. His account in her Love Bank is being drained. *How much longer can I put up with this?* she wonders.

Just as I sympathize with the woman's frustration, I sympathize with the man trapped in this situation. He does the best he can yet cannot meet his wife's emotional need for financial support. Is there an answer to this kind of impasse? Somehow, he must increase his income without sacrificing time with his family. He can try to obtain a raise in pay or a job that pays more, or he may need to go through the trouble of a career change. The following story illustrates how one couple solved this problem.

When Sean and Mindy came to me for counseling, Sean's career had reached a plateau. He had advanced about as far as he could with the company where he worked. I saw Mindy first, and she broke into tears. "I suppose I shouldn't feel this way, but I am losing respect for Sean. He can't earn enough to pay our bills, and now he wants me to go back to work to make up the difference. With the children so young, I just don't want to do that."

"What about cutting back on expenses?" I asked.

"As far as I'm concerned, we're at the bare minimum now. I suppose we shouldn't have bought a bigger house, but now we're in it. And we could never get along without a second car. We just live too far out for me to be home alone without some kind of transportation."

I pulled out the only other card in my hand. "Perhaps Sean could earn quite a bit more if he finished his education—I believe you said he had two years left. Would you be willing to go to work to help him?"

"Well, I suppose I could—just so it wouldn't be forever," Mindy replied. "I'll talk to Sean and see what he thinks."

Within a few weeks, Sean and Mindy had things worked out. She had found a full-time job, and his company had allowed him to take a part-time position so he could attend college and finish his degree.

Their new plan saved their marriage. Mindy was pleased to see Sean trying to improve his income-earning potential, and she did not mind the sacrifice because she knew it wouldn't be permanent. Ironically enough, Mindy loved her job so much that she chose to continue working even after Sean had completed school and began earning enough to support the family. In the end, she gained respect for her husband *and* a valued career for herself.

If a husband's income is truly insufficient for a family's basic needs, he should try to improve his job skills. His employer may pay for the additional training while he is still working full-time, or he may get financial help from social agencies. But if support for his improvement is not available, his wife may decide to go to work to make it possible. I have found that most women are willing to work to help support the family if it is a *temporary* solution to a financial crisis. This temporary sacrifice can actually prove to be a powerful builder of rapport and affection in the marriage. When a husband and a wife work together toward a common goal, their interests are much more likely to overlap, and their conversations will become more interesting to each other. In short, they become a winning team, and players on a winning team usually like and respect one another.

A Radical Solution

Having counseled so many couples like Sean and Mindy, I've become aware of how little it costs to be happy. As a short-term measure, while education is being completed, couples can learn to cut their costs to the bone, especially when they don't have children. Once the changes are made, they're often amazed at how satisfied they are living on a shoestring.

When I first met Sarah and Jim, they had set themselves adrift and seemed headed for the financial rocks. Both worked full-time, but things they bought with their dual incomes gave them little pleasure. They became addicted to drugs and alcohol, abandoned their moral values, and seemed destined to self-destruct.

When they came to see me, I convinced them that they both needed a new direction in life and that a college education was a good place to find that direction. They had only one problem—they were accustomed to living on their combined income of nine thousand dollars a month, and they could never earn that much and attend school too.

I suggested a radical solution. "Have you ever lived on less than two thousand dollars a month?" I asked. (Since I counseled this couple many years ago, I have adjusted the dollar amount to take inflation into account. So back then, the amount was much less.)

They looked at each other and started to laugh. "No one can live on two thousand dollars a month."

"Oh, on the contrary, most people in the world live on less than a fraction of that much. You might find it interesting to experiment and see how the rest of the world does it."

The two of them left my office that day still chuckling and shaking their heads, but I had planted the seed. It took them several weeks to make the decision, and I am certain they thought the experiment would become something like joining VISTA or the Peace Corps. Nonetheless, we worked out the following monthly budget:

Housing and utilities	$600
Groceries	$400
Clothes	$100
Miscellaneous and emergencies	$700
Total	$1,800

They rented a single room near the university they attended. They did almost all their cooking with a makeshift stove. Because they had sold their cars, they rode the bus or biked to school and work. They bought nourishing but inexpensive food. All their clothing purchases were made at thrift shops. They already had furniture. The money from the sale of their cars and unneeded possessions went into savings.

Each of them worked only fifteen hours a week to earn the one thousand dollars they needed. Now that they could not afford the drugs or alcohol that had been ruining their lives, they had to overcome their addictions. They even had to give up smoking. When they completed their education, they still had money in their savings account.

As part of their overall plan to reform their lives, they agreed to schedule fifteen hours a week for undivided attention. For the first time in their marriage, they deliberately met each other's intimate emotional needs for affection, intimate conversation, sexual fulfillment, and recreational companionship.

In their case, their education didn't help them earn more income. But the education, combined with meeting each other's intimate emotional needs, vastly increased their quality of life from what it had been. Their marriage blossomed because of the attention they gave each other. Even though Sarah and Jim were spending a fraction of what they had spent before, they were undeniably happy. Their marriage, about to end in divorce when I first saw them, now flourished. This change took place *while* they were living on one thousand dollars a month.

It's possible to live on much less than we do and be happier for doing it. I am certainly not trying to convince you that you should live on less than two thousand dollars a month. But almost any family *can* live comfortably on less than they presently spend. I simply want you to consider the idea that spending less may be much easier for you than earning more.

Many women I've counseled were sacrificing the fulfillment of their important emotional need for financial support by creating a standard of living they could not afford. Many of the men were working themselves into an early grave by trying to provide what their families could do without. Sometimes the cost of high living standards is at the expense of life's most valuable treasures.

If your career prevents you from having the time to meet each other's intimate and important emotional needs, keeping you from giving each other fifteen hours of undivided attention, what value is it? Wouldn't a career and a budget to match make you happier if it gave you time to meet those needs for each other?

After considering what I have just written, you might want to modify your needs budget. Do you really need everything that was included in that budget for you to be happy?

Together you may prove the truth of this saying: "When it comes to money and marriage, less may be more."

QUESTIONS FOR HIM

1. When you first married, did you think your wife would expect you to support her financially? Did you expect her to work? Do you know if this is an important emotional need for her today?

2. Do you think your wife is satisfied with the money you can presently earn working a normal workweek?

3. If this is an important emotional need for your spouse, have you ever considered retraining so that you could qualify for a job that pays more? Would cutting household expenses accomplish the same objective?

QUESTIONS FOR HER

1. Do you have financial support as a top emotional need? If so, have you thought much about your husband's income and how it affects your standard of living? How do you feel about it?

2. Would you feel comfortable sharing with him any negative feelings you may have about his level of income? Have you shared these feelings in the past?

3. If this is a top need for you, are you willing to reduce your standard of living so your husband's income alone will support you?

TO CONSIDER TOGETHER

1. What is your current standard of living? Do you both feel happy with it? Do you really have enough money to meet it?

2. Use the Financial Support Inventory, found in appendix D, to create a needs budget, a wants budget, and an affordable budget.

3. Should you make some changes? Would retraining help? Would reducing your standard of living help? Decide together how to implement needed changes.

4. Are you currently scheduling fifteen hours a week to meet each other's intimate emotional needs? If not, doing so would greatly increase your overall quality of life.

TEN

Domestic Support

Phil was a prosperous young bachelor. His job paid well. Because he had made a substantial down payment, his car payments were low. His apartment was pleasant, nicely furnished, and well situated. He had dated a number of women before he met Charlene, but she turned out to be different—special. They became best friends, and after about eight months of dating, he asked her to marry him.

The wedding took place in October. At first, they lived in his apartment, but that was just to give them time to finish accumulating the money to put down on a house. Because Charlene had a good job too, they had no trouble pooling their resources to become homeowners.

The next summer they found the place they wanted, and they moved by September. Phil relished many of the responsibilities of owning a home—caring for the yard, making repairs, installing new fixtures, and so forth.

Everything went well until their first child arrived. Then Charlene decided to cut back to part-time work. That reduced their income at a time when their expenses escalated. Phil took a second job to compensate for the loss of Charlene's income. He found himself working twelve-hour days, first as manager of his department, then as a part-time bookkeeper for another company.

At the end of five years, Phil and Charlene had three children. Phil still worked two jobs, but coming home from his second job, he found the demand greater than ever. Charlene still needed things fixed and sought help with the children. The lawn still needed mowing, and Charlene began to complain that their two-bedroom house was not large enough for their family.

Life, once so pleasant for Phil, rapidly became intolerable. He tried to escape by watching television and surfing the internet, but that didn't work well because Charlene continually asked him to get up and help her around the house. Next, he started staying at work after quitting time and hanging around with some of his coworkers, but that only aroused Charlene's ire. She felt hurt and angry when he didn't come home in time to help. When they sat down to talk with each other, which wasn't very often, Charlene used the opportunity to express her intense dissatisfaction with his lack of help with their children and household tasks. And when he came home from work late, which was almost always, Charlene was in no mood to make love with him. Eventually, he stopped coming home altogether.

A Domestic Bliss Fantasy

Unmet emotional needs often trigger fantasies, and the need for domestic support is no exception. Let's say the fantasy of a stereotypical man goes something like this: His home life is free of stress and worry. After work each day, his wife greets him lovingly, and their well-behaved children are also glad to see him. He enters the comfort of a well-maintained home as his wife urges him to relax before having dinner, the aroma of which he can already smell wafting from the kitchen. Conversation at dinner is enjoyable and free of conflict. Later the family goes out together for an early evening stroll, and he returns to put the children to bed with no hassle or fuss. Then he and his wife relax and talk together, watch a little television, and, at a reasonable hour, go to bed to make love.

Some wives may have laughed (or become enraged) as they read the above scenario, but I assure you that a revolution in male attitudes toward housework that was supposed to have taken place—with men pitching in to take an equal share of the household chores—has not necessarily changed their emotional needs. Many of the men I counsel still tell me in private that they need domestic support as much as ever.

If behavior is any measure of attitude change, I don't see much change in the way men really feel about housework. They may talk a lot about how unfair it is to expect women to do most of the chores, but when it comes to actually sharing the burden, their wives know that it's mostly talk. Several research reports I've read recently indicate that husbands in dual-career marriages contribute only about 10 percent more to household and childcare tasks than husbands whose wives are stay-at-home moms. I read that same statistic about thirty years ago. Much has been written about this imbalance, but as most wives with careers and children will testify, little has been done about it.

There are several theories as to why this imbalance occurs. One theory that seems reasonable is that men are simply not wired for domestic tasks. They don't see the mess and don't hear the children running wild. When they do volunteer to help, they don't really get much accomplished, at least from their wives' perspectives. They just don't have much of an instinct for household tasks.

But there's another theory that I propose: men tend to have an emotional need for domestic support. When a man's wife manages the household and children, her actions make massive deposits into his Love Bank. But that need and the lifestyle challenges of families created in the past sixty years have produced an almost impossible burden on the wives of these men. They simply can't meet that need the way the husband wants it to be met. They need their husband's help.

Furthermore, these lifestyle challenges have created the same need in women, especially career women. They have a need for domestic support too.

In the last chapter, I asked women with the emotional need for financial support if they would marry a man who refused to earn an income. I've found that most men would marry a woman they love even if she let him know unequivocally that he could not expect her to contribute to the family budget (I'm included in that group). Most women, on the other hand, would not marry a man who expected to be unemployed throughout his entire lifetime.

Technically, that test can be given to determine the existence of any emotional need. Would you have married your spouse knowing that they would be unwilling to provide any affection to you? How about sex? Or intimate conversation? Or honesty and openness? Add to that the caveat that whatever it is, you can't get it outside of marriage either—your spouse is the only ethical source. What can you do *without*? Whatever it might be, it's not an important emotional need for you.

To help spouses identify their top five emotional needs from the list of ten, I tell them that they can have only one need from the list that's met consistently and effectively by their spouse. All others will go completely unmet. What would that one need be? Most tell me they wouldn't have married someone who met only one need, but I encourage them to humor me by trying to determine what that need would be.

After identifying that need, I ask them to imagine having two needs met but no others. What would their second choice be? I then go on until they have identified their top five emotional needs. In most marriages, the top five of the husband are very different from the top five of the wife.

So this test can be given to determine the need for domestic support. Would a man who has this as a top emotional need marry a woman who is unwilling to manage the housework or childcare? For him, it's one of his most important emotional needs, which means that it makes massive Love Bank deposits when met and is very frustrating when unmet.

Time again for a disclaimer. Not all husbands identify this need among their top five. In fact, I've known many women who rank it in *their* top five emotional needs. I'm sure there are many couples who are happy with the husband managing the household and childcare tasks. As always, it's up to you and your spouse to discover your emotional needs and then communicate them to each other. You may find that this need simply isn't an issue for you. I've seen that happen many times.

You may object to my test for determining this need by arguing that domestic support isn't an all-or-nothing proposition. It isn't something that only one person does. It should be something done together.

I heartily agree. I propose the test simply as a way for me to demonstrate the existence of a need. My point is that many men would have a very difficult time living with a wife who does not take responsibility for childcare or housework. Women, on the other hand, may find such a husband frustrating, but his lack of domestic support wouldn't necessarily deplete their Love Banks to the same degree. In fact, many women in very successful marriages complain about their husbands' unwillingness to help out more around the house.

The Fair Division of Labor Dilemma

Sixty years ago, it was more common for the average wife to be a stay-at-home mom or homemaker. But things have changed. Today the average wife is employed full-time. In fact, there are now more women in the workplace than men. As would be expected, with this shift, the division of domestic responsibilities has become a major source of marital conflict. Not only has the shift changed the dynamics of a husband's need for domestic support, but now more women also sense that need themselves. The "man's fantasy" that I described in the last section is the "woman's fantasy" as well. They both want to relax after a stressful day at work.

Is the need for domestic support deep-seated and instinctive for men, or is it driven by the demands of a career? Do women who are exhausted by the demands of their careers feel the same need for domestic support as their husbands?

Consider this common situation. The husband and the wife both return home from work at about six and eat a takeout dinner with their two children. There are dishes to be cleaned up, laundry to be washed and put away, carpets to be vacuumed, children to be bathed, and stories to be read to the children before they go to sleep. But as soon as dinner is over, the husband sits down to watch TV.

There is almost unanimous agreement that a husband and a wife should share household and childcare responsibilities if they both work full-time. But they usually don't have the same sense of urgency about caring for the home and children. She wants domestic tasks completed, and he has a need for her to complete them. With these realities facing the average dual-career couple, how can they come to a fair division of labor?

When it comes to making any behavioral change, motivation is almost everything. If the change is enjoyable to the one who makes it or if there is a reward for making the change, you can safely assume "mission accomplished."

But if the change is unpleasant and if there is no reward, all the promises to change will likely lead to broken promises.

A Plan for the Fair Division of Labor

With motivational realities in mind, I've designed a way for dual-income couples, and even stay-at-home spouses who would like more help from their partners, to apply tried and proven motivational principles to solve their fair division of labor dilemma.

My plan actually works for spouses who have an emotional need for domestic support and those who do not. The difference is what they expect to give and receive while completing the assignments of the plan. A husband or a wife with an emotional need for domestic support will offer less support but will enjoy the support they receive much more than the spouse without the need. I use that observation to create a plan that makes them both happy.

This may look daunting at first because it involves so much thought, analysis, and preparation, but those who have followed this plan have consistently told me that it solved their problem once and for all when their previous attempts had failed. You will find that it's definitely worth your effort.

Step 1: Identify Your Household and Childcare Tasks

Make a list of all your household and childcare tasks. The list should (1) name each responsibility, and (2) briefly describe what must be done and when it must be accomplished. We'll call this your master list.

Both spouses should add items to this list, and it will take several days to think of everything. You will add to it each day as you find yourself accomplishing various tasks or wanting them accomplished.

Examples of tasks on the list are as follows:

Cleaning up the breakfast dishes—clear off the breakfast table every morning; wash, dry, and put away all the breakfast dishes and utensils that were used to prepare and eat the breakfast.
Feeding the cat—put cat food and water in the cat's dishes at 8:00 a.m. and 5:00 p.m.

When you have finished your list, both of you should be satisfied that it includes all the household and childcare responsibilities that you share. You may have as many as a hundred items listed. Just this part of the exercise alone will help you understand what you're up against regarding the work that you feel must be done.

Step 2: Assume Responsibility for Some Tasks

There are some tasks that you enjoy doing by yourself. Or you don't think your spouse will get them done the way you want them done—you'd rather do them yourself. Those tasks should be taken from your master list and placed on two new lists, one titled "His Responsibilities" and the other titled "Her Responsibilities."

If both you and your spouse want to take responsibility for the same items, you can either take turns doing them or arbitrarily divide them between the two of you. But you must approve each other's selections before they become that spouse's final responsibility. If one of you does not feel that the other will perform the task well enough, you might give each other a trial period to demonstrate competence. Once you have taken responsibility for an item, your spouse should be able to hold you accountable for doing it according to their expectations.

Step 3: Assign Tasks That You Are Willing to Do Only if They Are Done Together

Now you have three lists: (1) his responsibilities, (2) her responsibilities, and (3) what remains on your master list—the list of household and childcare tasks that neither of you has signed up for yet.

There are many household and childcare tasks that you would not enjoy doing by yourself, but you would enjoy doing them together. You may find that putting away the dishes after they have been washed in the dishwasher is more fun when you do it together (Joyce puts away the dishes and I put away the silverware). The same can be said for spending time with your children. You might enjoy it far more if your spouse is with you. These tasks, if agreed to with enthusiasm, should be taken from your master list and placed on a fourth list titled "Our Responsibilities."

Tasks on this list have already been clearly defined. You have described what is to be done and when it is to be done. But certain aspects of the tasks may need to be modified if both spouses are to enjoy doing them together.

Step 4: Decide Who Wants the Tasks Done the Most

If your master list still includes household and childcare tasks, they represent items that neither of you wants to do by yourself or together. So the next step is to decide who wants them done the most. You do that by rating how important it is to you to have each task accomplished (use a scale from 0 to 5, with 0 indicating no importance and 5 indicating most important). Each of you rate each task and then discuss your ratings with each other.

Examples of items on the list are as follows:

Cleaning up the kitchen after breakfast—clear off the breakfast table every morning; put the breakfast dishes and utensils in the dishwasher; put them away after they have been washed: Becky (4); John (2).

Feeding the cat—put cat food and water in the cat's dishes at 8:00 a.m. and 5:00 p.m.: John (5); Becky (3).

You may have trouble being honest when completing this assignment because you may suspect that I will be assigning the remaining tasks to the one who wants them done the most. When Becky sees that John rates cleaning up the kitchen after breakfast as 2, she might change her rating to a 1. Seeing her rating of 1, he might change his rating to a 0 to make sure she ends up with the responsibility.

But I want accurate numbers from each of you because I will encourage you to eliminate some of the items completely if both of your ratings are very low. Why do something if it's not wanted very much by either of you? How would you feel if the task were not done at all? That should determine your rating.

Step 5: Assign the Remaining Tasks to Who Wants Them Done the Most

You are motivated to complete the tasks on your individual lists and your joint list of responsibilities because you enjoy doing them or prefer to do them. But you are not as motivated to complete the remaining tasks. So to whom should responsibility be assigned?

As you may have suspected, I suggest that these tasks be assigned to the person who wants them done the most because that person would be the most motivated to do them. It's a reasonable solution, since to do otherwise would force responsibility on the one who cares least about the completion.

At this point in my plan, most women react with alarm. "I know how this will turn out," they complain. "All of these tasks will end up on my list. My husband could care less about keeping our home neat and clean."

Wives who are employed full-time want many of these tasks completed but don't have the time or energy to complete them. So they want their husbands, who are also tired at the end of the day, to share the load. From their perspective, it's a fair division of labor to divide these tasks equally when neither spouse wants to do them. It's unfair for the wife to be engaged in a wide assortment of household and childcare tasks while her husband surfs the web. She's the one who wants the work done, but she feels he should share responsibility for doing it, even if he doesn't want to do it.

As most wives have discovered by now, wanting a husband to take responsibility for tasks that only the wife wants completed doesn't work. Since he's not motivated, he doesn't do them. She can call him irresponsible and lazy all she wants, but in the end, either she completes the tasks herself or they won't be done.

Telling someone that it's their responsibility to do something that you want done isn't motivating. It's usually demotivating. It's likely to lead to an argument rather than to the help an exhausted wife needs from her husband.

I want her to get the help she needs from her husband, but the way she goes about getting that help must motivate him. Trust me. I don't want to leave wives burdened with a list of household tasks that allows them only three hours of sleep each night. On the contrary, the rest of my plan will give them a full eight hours. But the plan is realistic by assigning undesirable tasks to the one most motivated to do them—the one who wants them done the most.

Step 6: Get Help from Others, Eliminate Tasks, and Get Eight Hours of Sleep Every Night

When a spouse first sees their complete list of responsibilities—those they have chosen to do and those they're left with doing because they want them done the most—they will feel overwhelmed. So I help them think of ways to shift some of the responsibility to hired help or to the children. The need for domestic support isn't necessarily met by actually doing the household tasks. It's met by seeing to it that they're done—managing the household.

Children should definitely get in on the act. They should be assigned some of the tasks on a list to relieve the burden. But be sure that you do not assign your children tasks that both you and your spouse find too unpleasant to shoulder. It doesn't build character to give your kids jobs that you hate to do; it builds resentment. Your assignment should also be discussed first with your children. Have them choose tasks from your list of household responsibilities. Make lists for them as well as for you and your spouse. There will be plenty to keep them busy.

If the choice is available to you, shifting some household tasks to hired help would obviously cause a shift in budget priorities. But if you're able to make it work—either regularly or occasionally—it can relieve a great deal of burden.

After you have assigned tasks to your children or others, I strongly encourage you to consider the possibility that many of the tasks left on your list may not need to be done as often or at all.

Some women I've counseled have felt compelled to wash, sort, and put away all the family's clothes every night all by themselves. It bothers them to see unwashed clothes in the hamper. I strongly suggest to these women that they set aside one day a week to do all the washing, sorting, and distributing of clothes, usually Saturday morning. And by making this a family project in which the children, and often the husband, participate, the wife can get the sleep she needs during the week.

My plan for a fair division of labor requires eight hours of sleep every night for both the husband and the wife. It also requires fifteen hours of undivided attention for romantic dates each week. That means that your final list of tasks must give you the freedom and the opportunity to rise above mundane tasks to engage in high-priority goals. That may require you to eliminate some of your tasks altogether. What happens if no one does them? Would anyone but you care? Maybe you don't have the time to complete tasks that are important only to you.

But before you make those decisions, there are two more steps left in my plan. Steps 7 and 8 are designed to motivate a husband or wife to help with tasks that are not already on the "Our Responsibilities" list.

Step 7: Indicate How Happy You Would Be with Your Spouse's Help

Up to this point, the assignment of household responsibilities has been fair. You divided them according to a willingness to do them and according to a desire to have them accomplished. This division has met a spouse's emotional need for domestic support.

There's hardly a wife who wants the plan to end there, however. She wants help with those responsibilities that remain on her list when she can't get outside help, and she is too exhausted to do it by herself. She wants that help from her husband. Trying to *force* him to help by being disrespectful or appealing to his guilt doesn't work because it's not motivational. But there's something else she can do that will motivate most husbands—she can use the Love Bank illustration to explain how happy it would make her to have his help.

You already have numbers assigned to each task—the importance of the task to each of you. Now I want you to assign one more number. This time write a number indicating how many love units you think would be deposited if your spouse were to help you or would do the task for you. Use a scale from 0 to 5, with 0 indicating that you would experience no pleasure (no love units) and 5 indicating that you would experience maximum pleasure and would be eternally grateful (unlimited love units).

A wife is not the only one who should rate appreciation levels on her list of responsibilities. A husband should rate them on his list as well.

Step 8: Help Your Spouse Where Your Effort Is Most Appreciated

If these ratings are accurate, it means that whenever you complete a task for your spouse rated 4 or 5, or even help them with it, you will be making a very large Love Bank deposit. Your help will make your spouse happy, and it will be greatly appreciated. Knowing this may change an otherwise unpleasant task into a very enjoyable one for you. It may be the motivation you need to share the burden of household and childcare tasks.

If cooking dinner or picking up socks makes large Love Bank deposits, why not do these things? As a matter of fact, if meeting any of the emotional needs I've described in this book really does create the feeling of love, why would anyone resist doing them? This is not only an act of caring love but also an act of supreme wisdom. By doing for each other what is most appreciated, you will have a much greater incentive to meet each other's emotional needs. When you do that for each other, you will have what few marriages have, the feeling of love throughout your entire lives together.

How does the need for domestic support affect this step in the plan? When either you or your spouse has a need for domestic support, you will enjoy having your spouse engage in household and childcare tasks that have been assigned to them and you will be frustrated when that doesn't happen. This is what it means to have an emotional need for domestic support. So if the husband has a need for domestic support, he will ask his wife to help him with his list of responsibilities. If the wife has a need for domestic support, she will ask him to help her in the same way. This is where the need for domestic support becomes most obvious. You meet that need for each other by helping complete tasks rated 4 or 5 on each other's lists.

But let me repeat another important concept that I have mentioned earlier: *don't waste your time on needs of lesser importance*. If your spouse doesn't appreciate the help you offer, put your energy into meeting other, more important emotional needs. Don't do housework for your spouse if it is not appreciated. Remember, whatever is on your spouse's list is your spouse's responsibility, not yours. If your effort to relieve your spouse of a particular task really doesn't seem to have much effect on your spouse, don't waste your time. Put your effort into another task that is more appreciated.

Your spouse's response to your help should prove whether or not love units are being deposited. If your spouse thanks you when you perform the task and expresses their appreciation with affection, you know you are on the right track. But if your spouse ignores you after performing one of these tasks, you are not making Love Bank deposits for some reason. In that case, go back to your spouse's original list of tasks and pick something else to do that has a greater impact.

Just because you decide to help your spouse with one of their responsibilities does not make it *your* responsibility. Actually, that's a very important way to look at meeting emotional needs in general. If meeting any emotional need is viewed as a responsibility, then it is not appreciated as much when it's met. Only when the meeting of emotional needs is seen as a gift—as an act of caring love—does it have the maximum impact on the Love Bank. If either you or your spouse takes the meeting of an emotional need for granted, the effect will tend to be greatly diluted.

I must make one final point. If knowing that your spouse appreciates your help doesn't make the task enjoyable for you, you'll never get into the habit of helping them with that task. And deposits in their Love Bank will be offset by withdrawals from yours. So when you help your spouse with tasks from their list of responsibilities, you must figure out a way to help them that is enjoyable for you.

To summarize, when creating a plan for a fair division of household responsibilities, depositing the most love units and avoiding their withdrawal should be your guide. Assume household responsibilities that you enthusiastically accept or want accomplished more than your spouse does. Then find tasks that you would both enjoy doing if you did them together. The remaining tasks that no one claims should go to the spouse who wants them done the most. Finally, if either spouse appreciates help with tasks on their list, and that appreciation is motivation enough for their spouse to enjoy doing the tasks, they should provide as much help as they can.

This approach to the division of household and childcare tasks guarantees mutual care, especially when you feel like being uncaring. It prevents you from trying to gain at your spouse's expense and from trying to force your spouse into an unpleasant way of life with you. It points you in a direction where both of you will find happiness, fulfillment, and, best of all, the feeling of romantic love for each other.

QUESTIONS FOR HER

1. What do you think of the fair division of labor plan that's offered in this chapter? Would it help you organize household and childcare tasks and discuss the best ways to accomplish them?

2. Do you feel that your husband expects too much of you or that you expect too much of yourself when it comes to completing household and childcare tasks? Does he use demands, disrespect, or anger? Or does he request help and then show appreciation?

3. If your husband identifies domestic support as one of his emotional needs, how do you react to the idea of managing the household tasks rather than trying to do them all yourself or trying to force him to do some of them?

QUESTIONS FOR HIM

1. What do you think of the fair division of labor plan that's offered in this chapter? When you don't provide as much help as your wife would like, do you feel guilty? Or do you feel that household and childcare tasks should be her responsibility?

2. How does your wife try to motivate you to help her with household and childcare tasks? Does she use demands, disrespect, or anger? Or does she request help and then show appreciation?

3. Have you ever identified domestic support as an emotional need? How does that affect your expectations of your wife and household management?

TO CONSIDER TOGETHER

1. Discuss the ways you have burdened each other with responsibilities:

    a. with a standard of living that requires more time at work than you like

    b. with children's activities that are more time-consuming than you anticipated

    c. with volunteer work that takes time away from your family

    d. with hobbies and recreational interests that separate you from each other

2. If a need for domestic support has been identified by either spouse, follow the plan in this chapter to create a fair division of labor. Try it for a few weeks before you judge its value.

3. Discuss this statement taken from the chapter: "If meeting any emotional need is viewed as a responsibility, then it is not appreciated as much when it's met. Only when the meeting of emotional needs is seen as a gift—as an act of caring love—does it have the maximum impact on the Love Bank" (p. 139).

ELEVEN

Family Commitment

Ann and Terry met in their early thirties. Both felt ready to settle down. Their relationship was very good, with one exception: Terry did not care for Ann's parents. He felt they had too much to say about how Ann conducted her life. Their unsolicited advice annoyed him a great deal. Ann felt bad about this, but she knew other couples who had problems that seemed worse to her. She and Terry got along so well in every other area that she decided to try to live with the problem. *Maybe, in time, it will work itself out*, she told herself.

Terry's eagerness to get away from Ann's family dampened the wedding celebration considerably. Ann hardly had time to even greet her relatives before her new husband whisked her away on the honeymoon trip.

During their first year of marriage, Ann tried to interest Terry in her family get-togethers but to no avail. She soon learned that he would have little to do with his own parents, much less spend time with hers.

The problem didn't "work itself out," and after their two children arrived, Ann realized that Terry's lack of family commitment extended to them as well. When they were babies, Ann wrote it off as a typical male attitude. *He'll be more interested when they get older*, she thought.

But Terry didn't become more interested. He had little time for the children, and when they clamored for his attention, he became irritable.

Finally, Ann quit hoping and admitted to herself that she had married a man who just wasn't family-oriented. She worried about what would happen to their children, who needed their dad.

The Need for a Strong Family Unit

The vast majority of women have a powerful instinct to create a family. When the family does arrive, many wives want their husbands to play a significant role in the moral and educational development of the children. The ideal scenario for a wife is to marry a man she can respect and who the children will respect and be guided by his influence.

In families in which the father takes little interest in the children's development, the mother tries desperately to motivate him to change. Maybe she buys him books on parenting and leaves them in convenient places. Perhaps she coaches him to attend seminars sponsored by the church or PTA. She may even ask him to talk with a family counselor in the hope that he can be inspired to greater interest and commitment. Her efforts are usually met with only partial success. More often she becomes frustrated by excuses, delays, and other unenthusiastic responses on her husband's part. Not uncommonly, such a mother starts looking to other men in her family or circle of friends to meet her need.

What does a woman really mean when she says she wants her children to "have a good father"? Behind that remark lie expectations of responsibilities she wants him to fulfill. Ironically enough, he might feel that those responsibilities conflict with his need for domestic support, which includes childcare. To deal with such a situation, the couple must achieve open communication in two important areas: time and training.

Parenting Takes Time—*Lots of Time*

A husband should devote time to his family. He can strengthen both his marriage and his ties with his children by developing what I call *quality family time*. This is not to be confused with childcare necessities for all parents—feeding, clothing, and watching over children to keep them safe. Those are domestic tasks that were discussed in the last chapter. Quality family time is when the family is together for the moral and educational development of the children.

I have already recommended that a husband and a wife schedule fifteen hours each week for giving undivided attention to each other. That time is to be spent meeting each other's intimate emotional needs so that their romantic love for each other remains strong. When I made that recommendation, you probably thought it couldn't be done, but with a goal of keeping your marriage secure, you may have found a way to schedule the time each week. If so, you have rearranged your priorities, spending your precious time on what means the most to you.

But now I will make a second recommendation that will require another rearrangement of priorities. I recommend an additional fifteen hours a week for quality family time. Without a doubt, the hours spent with your children are some of the most important hours of the week. And if you want to influence your children, training them to become successful adults, time together is crucial. But do you actually have that much time left in your schedule?

Consider your total time each week. You have 168 hours (24 hours a day, 7 days a week). For 8 hours of sleep each night (don't risk your health), take away 56 hours, leaving 112 hours. If you estimate the time it takes to get ready for work in the morning and ready for bed at night to be another 12 hours, that leaves 100 hours. Your job, including getting there and returning home again, should not take more than 50 hours a week (if you work more than that, you will not achieve your most important objectives in life). After carving out time for all these things, there are still 50 hours left for you to schedule. You have 15 hours for undivided attention and another 15 hours for quality family time, leaving you with 20 hours for everything else you want to accomplish: household and childcare tasks, church activities, gardening, hobbies, or just sitting at home relaxing while reading a book.

A time budget (weekly schedule) is like a financial budget. It helps you keep your priorities straight. If you don't budget your money, you will make so many low-priority purchases that you will have no money left for things that are truly important to you. The same is true with a time budget. If you don't schedule your week with your highest priorities in mind, you'll run out of time before you can accomplish them.

To make this change for your family, you will need to eliminate some activities that are currently in your schedule. But ask yourself if the activities you will be eliminating are more important than your care for each other and your care for your children.

Once you've carved out the hours in your schedule, you'll be ready to consider what you will be doing during this time. Remember, the purpose of quality family time is the *moral and educational development of your children.* Among the most important lessons taught to children are thoughtfulness and how to care for each other. So your activities should focus attention on helping each other, showing a cooperative spirit. Keep your family together as a unit during this time and make it fun for your children, not a time of drudgery.

What should you do during quality family time? Consider activities such as these:

- meals together as a family
- attending church services
- family meetings
- going on walks and bike rides
- playing board games together
- reading to the children before bedtime
- helping the children with homework
- family projects and household tasks (be certain these are fun for the children as you work on them together as a family)

You may find that making room in your schedule for quality family time doesn't require the elimination of activities but rather their modification. For example, if your family currently has meals on the run, with everyone grabbing a bite to eat separately, start having your meals together. Instead of activities that separate your family members, try to arrange to do things as a family.

One of the biggest consumers of parental time can be after-school sports, music, and theater. They are usually spent one child at a time, with little opportunity for family participation and influence. Don't let these activities prevent you from providing your family with your valuable influence. After scheduling time for undivided attention and quality family time, use only the time that you have remaining for these after-school activities that separate the family. Athletic, musical, and theatrical activities can be planned that keep the family together.

If you have children under the age of twelve, you will find it fairly easy to motivate them to spend time with you in this way. Once they reach their teens, however, they will begin to tax your ingenuity. Now they want to spend most of their time with their friends; your family begins to see less and less of them. To compensate, develop well-planned events aimed at teens; otherwise they will express their dissatisfaction clearly and with great vigor!

If your children have grown up with such family time, it should not be too difficult to motivate them to continue the practice. That doesn't mean you will not be challenged by teens who have other plans, but with some more thought and perhaps more expense in your plans, you can develop something your teens will *agree* to continue. But if you try to start family time during your children's teen years, they may not agree at all to such an arrangement. I've witnessed such heated arguments on this issue between parents and children that I have recommended that the family forget about quality family time. They have simply, though sadly, lost their opportunity.

Most educators realize that children are easier to influence than teens or adults. Take a page from their book, and if your children are still young, make the most of your ability to mold them with quality moral standards and life principles that can benefit them for years. Keep in mind the goal of training your child "on the way they should go" (Prov. 22:6), with their future needs in mind. If you take family time seriously during your children's early growth stages, you will be far less likely to find yourself in trouble later.

Do you want your children's moral development to be dictated by their peers or by you as parents? Most parents want both, if their friends share the same moral values that they hope to create in their children. But the only way that can happen is if parents help their children choose their friends with morality in mind. Without quality time with their children, parents have much less influence on who their children's friends will be and what moral values those friends have. Friends often have more influence than you have as parents, especially as children age. So it's very important to align their friends' values with your own.

Parenting Takes Training—*Lots of Training*

If you wish to parent your children well, you also need to face the fact that you will need some training in this skill. No one is born knowing how to care for a child.

Hundreds of books on parenting appear on bookstore and library shelves each year, and countless seminars try to explain how to train children. These resources abound with information on everything from toilet training to enforcing bedtimes. But the following are a few basic guidelines for fathers that most mothers would enthusiastically endorse.

Learn How to Reach Agreement

A man should never ignore his wife's opinions regarding child training. She needs him to join her in the moral and educational development of their children—not take over. But many fathers don't know how to negotiate with their wives. They think conflicts in child training must be decided by force—which parent is strong enough to get their way? If the wife prevails, the husband steps back and lets her train the children by herself. If he prevails, he wants her to submit to his authority.

I've found that the wisest approach to child training is found through negotiation that leads to a mutually enthusiastic agreement. If a mother and a father agree on the rules their children will be expected to follow and agree on how to discipline them when those rules are not followed, they avoid the common mistakes most parents make. And by raising children with mutual agreement, a husband meets his wife's emotional need for family commitment.

If they can get away with it, children will divide and conquer. They make a deal with Mom to get around Dad and vice versa. To avoid that age-old strategy, when a child wants a privilege, Mom and Dad should consult together in private and give an agreed-upon answer.

In family after family, I have witnessed children successfully manipulate one parent who favors them. Dad favors Monika; Mom favors Jennifer. So Monika goes to Dad for money, and he tries to give it to her without Mom knowing. When Jennifer finds out about it, she demands the same treatment. Mom tries to make Dad give Jennifer the same amount of money, resulting in a deep wedge driven between husband and wife. To avoid this, all decisions should result from mutual agreement. If you and your spouse cannot agree, take *no* action until agreement is reached.

Reach agreement also on how you want to discipline your children. A joint opinion receives greater respect from children and carries more weight with them. When they know that you made the decision together, children are less likely to challenge it.

How a husband disciplines his children greatly affects his deposits in his wife's Love Bank. Women are very sensitive to inappropriate and overly harsh discipline. Often, they react as if the punishment the husband gave their children was given to them personally. Therefore, a husband should reach an enthusiastic agreement with his wife before either of them imposes any disciplinary solution. A method of discipline that a husband and a wife plan and implement jointly builds romantic love and reflects a husband's caring love for his wife's feelings when family commitment is her need.

On a related topic, discipline in blended families is especially important to agree upon before it's delivered. If not handled correctly, it often leads to divorce because of the massive Love Bank withdrawals that can result from unilateral decisions. The biological parent usually has a very heightened negative reaction to almost any discipline by the stepparent, and the stepchild often sees that and uses it against the stepparent. A relationship of hatred is often the result, with the stepchild becoming the stepparent's worst enemy. So to avoid that common outcome, I recommend that in blended families, the biological parents do almost all of the discipline. I also recommend that the stepparent make a special effort to care for the stepchild—to be the "giver of all good things." This not only helps make deposits in the biological parent's Love Bank but also helps avoid the very common tension between stepchildren and stepparents.

Learn How to Explain the Rules, Especially the Moral Value of Thoughtfulness

Children need to understand *why* they should do this or that. So parents should learn how to clearly and patiently explain the rules. Sometimes the conversation may go like this.

"Johnny, go upstairs and make your bed."

"Why?"

"Because we want you to grow up knowing how to keep yourself and your property neat and clean."

"Why?"

"Because being neat and clean makes the people you live with feel good and like living with you."

"Why?"

"Just go upstairs and make your bed *BECAUSE I SAID SO!*"

"Oh, okay."

You can easily understand the reaction to those seemingly endless questions, can't you? But the "because I said so" line doesn't benefit the child very much. When you feel frustrated, pulling out your parental muscle may work—you may get your child to take the appropriate action—but you may also have lost the opportunity to explain your rationale to your child. In situations such as these, you can subtly but clearly communicate your moral, ethical, and personal values, if you patiently answer the *why*s.

During your quality family time, the moral values of thoughtfulness and caring for each other should be expressed often. But when it comes time to explain why we all should be thoughtful toward each other, have an explanation for that basic value.

Jesus Christ summed up this very important moral value by saying, "Do to others what you would have them do to you, for this sums up the Law and the Prophets" (Matt. 7:12). For Christians, thoughtfulness is a very important goal in life. So if you raise your children as Christians, you can tell them that thoughtfulness toward others is what God wants from them. It's God's commandment.

It's a value that makes our lives much easier to live. Try raising children who have not been taught the value of thoughtfulness. They will make the job of raising them substantially more difficult. If you want to raise your children with relative peace and serenity and at the same time help ensure their success and happiness in life, teaching them to be thoughtful will carry you a long way toward those goals.

Learn How to Be Consistent

Children don't take long to discover that rules may depend on Mom's or Dad's mood. When Mom and Dad feel happy, children can do almost anything—run around the house, throw things, jump on the beds, yell at each other, and have a squirt-gun fight. But when Mom and Dad come home grumpy, watch out! Movement of any kind may be met with an angry outburst.

If rules are applied inconsistently, their meaning is lost on children. Instead of learning a moral principle, children focus their attention on a parent's mood. It becomes wrong for Johnny to yell at the top of his lungs only when Dad needs to concentrate on something or Mom doesn't feel up to par. Parents should make rules together and then stick to them, regardless of their mood.

Household rules should apply to everyone, and parents should lead by example. If you want your children to keep their rooms clean, make sure your room is clean. If you want your children to avoid arguing, don't argue with each other. Demonstrate how your children are to care for others in the way you care for each other.

Learn How to Punish Properly

Taking away privileges is the time-honored way parents punish older children. Incentives for good behavior should begin to replace punishment for bad behavior when training this age group.

By the time a child becomes a teenager, punishment should be completely phased out in favor of incentives or withholding privileges. Corporal punishment that is inflicted on older children can leave an emotional scar that persists throughout their lives.

I draw a distinction between punishment and withholding privileges. Punishment causes a child to suffer emotional or physical pain, while withholding privileges causes the temporary loss of pleasure. Having a cell phone is a privilege, so if it's taken away, the enjoyment associated with it is also temporarily removed. But it should be made clear when the cell phone is given to a child that it is on loan. Disobedience can require its return.

Children are encouraged to carry cell phones with them at school for safety reasons. But when they are at home, they should realize that its use depends on their behavior.

As you teach your children the moral value of thoughtfulness, you will find that inflicting punishment on them can be counterproductive to what you want your children to do. You don't want them punishing others, especially each other, so why are you punishing them? They will see the inconsistency immediately.

The very best way to train your children is by example. As you and your spouse demonstrate your care for each other by meeting each other's emotional needs and by protecting each other from your thoughtless habits, your children will learn what it means to be thoughtful. The quality family time you spend with your children teaching them important values, such as considering a person's feelings before acting, will go a long way toward raising children who need little or no discipline.

Learn How to Avoid Anger Entirely

Often, parents discipline their children in a state of anger. When they've had quite enough of a child's disobedience, they let loose. Just the other day I witnessed an example of such behavior in a shopping center parking lot. Inside the store, a child was kicking and screaming because his mother would not buy him a toy. The ruckus continued through the checkout line and all the way to their car. But after the mother had left the watchful eyes of guards and surveillance cameras, she began beating her son mercilessly. She wanted to let him know what a big mistake he had made, and I'm sure he got the message. But was it the right way for her to train her son? Did it teach him that it is okay to beat up someone when they upset you?

An angry outburst is temporary insanity, and the damage it can do is dangerous and unpredictable. If you were to watch a video recording of one of your angry outbursts, you'd see my point. But that's precisely what your children view when you use anger to punish them—they see an insane parent.

Even if angry outbursts were an effective way to keep your children in line, they're far too risky to use. Broken bones, permanent injury, and even death are the all-too-common consequences of this sad measure of discipline.

But discipline accompanied by anger doesn't usually work. Consider the disobedient child I witnessed in the store. I'm sure that his mother had beaten him many times before that incident. It wasn't working. That's because discipline given in anger is not carefully planned. It's impulsive, and it teaches a child that an angry outburst is an appropriate way to vent frustrations.

No child psychologist I have ever studied has recommended anger in any form as a tool for training a child. Control your anger *before* you discipline a child. By separating your emotion from the disciplinary action, you will become a far more effective disciplinarian.

Don't Let Parenting Compete with Romance

A common complaint I hear from new fathers is that the lover they married has been transformed into someone who has lost interest in romance. This is easy for a mother to do when overwhelmed with the new responsibility of raising a child. But it can be avoided if time for undivided attention is scheduled throughout a couple's child-rearing years.

Divorce is most common after the first year of marriage. But coming a close second is the year a couple has their first child. Isn't that sad? The cause of this tragic reality is usually a couple's failure to meet each other's intimate emotional needs. The priority of parenting competes with the priority of romance, and parenting wins.

When a wife is transformed from a lover into a mother, most men see only their loss of sexual fulfillment and recreational companionship as a factor in their marital collapse. But what can also happen is that the wife's needs for affection and intimate conversation are also unmet. The couple's loss of privacy and time to give each other undivided attention prevents the husband from meeting the wife's intimate emotional needs. Even if he becomes a good father, taking an active role in their child's personal development, it doesn't compensate for his failure to meet her intimate emotional needs. So when a woman wants her husband to spend every free moment caring for their children and ignores her own need for undivided attention, she runs a very high risk of falling out of love with him.

It's so important for parenting and romance to coexist in marriage that I've written *His Needs, Her Needs for Parents* to help couples balance their desire to be good parents with their need for intimacy. In it, I explain more fully many of the points I've made in this chapter. If you are new parents or are contemplating becoming parents, I highly recommend this book to you.

QUESTIONS FOR HIM

1. Have you committed yourself to your family? What does this mean in regard to quality family time and training in parenting skills?
2. Are you experiencing any problems with anger, administering punishment, consistency, or agreement with your wife on child discipline?
3. Are you overcome with responsibilities? How have you tried to communicate your juggling act to your wife? Does she seem to understand?

QUESTIONS FOR HER

1. Does your role as a mother interfere with your relationship with your husband? Has he ever complained about it?
2. Have you ever needed to encourage your husband to play a greater role in the moral and educational development of your children? If so, has it been effective? What could be more effective?
3. Have you and your husband made an effort to educate yourselves in parenting skills together? What are some parenting problems that you face that could use some attention?

TO CONSIDER TOGETHER

1. Share your answers to the above questions with each other honestly but respectfully.
2. What are the moral and educational goals you have for your children? Are you in agreement? How should your children be disciplined? Are you in agreement?
3. Schedule fifteen hours per week for quality family time. Plan activities during this time that help you achieve the moral and educational goals you have for your children. But don't let this time interfere with the time you schedule to give undivided attention to each other.

TWELVE

Admiration and Appreciation

Oh, Charles, thank you." Lori's eyes lit up with excitement. "What a wonderful painting! No one ever gave me his own original artwork before. You have so much talent."

"I don't know about that, Lori. I've got a long way to go."

"You underestimate yourself, honey. You are really good. I know enough about art to know that. You're a great artist, and I'm proud of you."

In Charles and Lori's courtship days, that would have been a typical conversation. She forever heaped praise on him, and it felt great. He'd never been complimented like that before.

But instead of developing a career in art, Charles decided, without discussing it together, to get a job in advertising instead. Based on the experience of his artist friends and colleagues, he felt that with a career in art he would never be able to support his family. And then, to make matters worse, his job required working long hours, often on weekends. By the time they had their first child, some of what had drawn Lori to Charles in the first place felt lost to her. Instead of being married to an artist, she was married to a man with a job she didn't respect who worked long hours away from home.

As Lori began to feel convinced that Charles would never develop his potential, her words of admiration tapered off and then ended altogether.

In their place, she used words of criticism to express her dissatisfaction with his career path and the lack of support he gave her at home. She was not happy with the way things were turning out for them. "Charles, we need to talk," Lori blurted out one evening after Charles had come home late again. "I'm not at all happy with how much time you're spending at work. We hardly ever see you."

"I wish I could be home more often, but we've had a sudden increase in advertising jobs that have to be done right away," he responded.

"You're putting all your time and energy into a career that means nothing to me. And you're not helping me raise our child!"

Charles was deeply offended by Lori's remarks. Here he was working hard for his family, and she didn't give him any credit for what he was doing on their behalf. So instead of saying anything more, he simply went to bed.

Two more children only made matters worse for them. Now, almost every conversation Lori had with Charles was filled with her criticism. To avoid those unpleasant interactions, he spent even more time away from home, sometimes sleeping overnight in his office.

Eventually, they both found their way to my office.

Admiration versus Appreciation

The words *admiration* and *appreciation* have different meanings. Admiration usually refers to your respect for someone, while appreciation is given in response to something that someone does for you. I admire and respect a great athlete who has broken a world record, but I appreciate the man who mows my lawn, even though I pay him, so that I don't have to do it myself.

But in spite of their different meanings, I've found that admiration and appreciation reflect a single emotional need in marriage. When Lori admired Charles for the artwork he was able to create, she also appreciated the painting he gave her. However, after he chose a career path she did not value and spent time away from his family to do it, she no longer admired him for the work he did, nor did she appreciate his effort in earning the income that job was providing.

In marriage, if you admire your spouse, you also tend to appreciate what they are doing for you. When you appreciate what your spouse does for you, you also tend to admire them.

Both admiration and appreciation should come from the heart. True, you can say words that express admiration or appreciation when, in fact, you do not admire or appreciate someone. But that's being dishonest. Since I place so much emphasis on honesty and openness in marriage, it wouldn't be consistent for me to encourage spouses to express their admiration and appreciation for each other when they aren't really felt.

Some might consider Lori's lack of appreciation for the income Charles was earning to be selfish. Like a child who doesn't get exactly what they want at the beginning of the day at Disney World and then pouts throughout the entire day, Lori couldn't seem to get beyond her dream of being married to a famous artist. Poor Charles. Once he gave up his ambition to paint for a living, nothing he did would seem to satisfy his wife.

But I wouldn't be so quick to judge Lori. Throughout this book, I have emphasized three important ingredients in meeting an emotional need: *quality*, *quantity*, and *mutuality*. Quality refers to the effectiveness of the way a need is met, quantity refers to how often it needs to be met, and mutuality is making sure that both spouses enjoy the experience when the need is met.

In Lori and Charles's case, the way he earned a living did not meet the quality or mutuality standards. The quality standard failed because the career he chose did not meet Lori's emotional need for financial support because she felt it was a waste of his artistic talent. She also didn't like how much time it took him away from their family. The mutuality standard failed because his career and the hours he put in to advance it were not mutually approved.

So if a spouse is to be admired and appreciated, they should be doing something that the other spouse values—something that meets their emotional need.

When Lori was dating Charles, she met one of his most important emotional needs: admiration. That admiration for his artistic talent rubbed off on almost everything else he did. She admired everything about him. That's an important reason he fell in love with her. But now that he is in a career she does not value and is taking very little part in helping her raise their children, she can't see anything of value in him. How can she give him accolades when she no longer feels any admiration toward anything he does? Her honest reaction is to be critical of him.

Criticism versus Complaints

Criticism is the opposite of admiration and appreciation. While admiration and appreciation can build a person up, criticism can tear them down.

A husband or a wife wants their spouse to be president of their fan club, not their worst critic, but some feel that it's their right and obligation to straighten out their spouse. So instead of showering them with accolades, they batter them with disapproval.

That's what Lori was doing to Charles. Not only was she failing to meet one of his top five emotional needs, but she was also compounding the error by treating him in a very disrespectful way. Instead of making massive Love Bank deposits with admiration for what he was doing for their family, she was making massive withdrawals with criticism.

Please understand, I do not recommend sweeping marital problems under the rug. I'd be the first to encourage spouses to express their grievances to each other. But doing so disrespectfully is ineffective and very damaging to a relationship, especially if a spouse has a need for admiration.

I draw a distinction between a criticism and a complaint. A complaint is the expression of a problem that you would like to solve. For example, "I have been feeling sexually frustrated lately, and I'd like to make love to you more often." This is a complaint.

A criticism, on the other hand, adds disrespect to the complaint. "You have certainly been a sexual disappointment to me. I had no idea you would turn out to be such a lousy lover." This added judgment changes the complaint into a criticism.

Which of the two expressions of need has the greatest chance of finding a resolution? One places the problem on the docket for discussion and negotiation. The other sets the stage for a fight.

While admiration may be difficult to express honestly in a marriage when everything seems to be turning out badly, don't make the mistake of making massive Love Bank withdrawals due to disrespect. If you have a complaint, get it out on the table, but keep your critical judgments to yourself.

A Plan to Create Greater Admiration and Appreciation

Lori wanted to be an admiring wife, but she didn't know how to do it honestly. So I offered her a plan that would help her give her husband compliments when he deserved them while at the same time turning her criticisms into complaints.

Sometimes a marriage can be so unsuccessful that spouses stop looking for the value in it. They want to get away from it so badly that they convince themselves there is nothing to respect in each other. But that's an illusion. The truth is that, regardless of the struggles you might be facing, there is value in everyone, especially your spouse.

So I encouraged Lori to start looking for value in Charles. As she thought of what he did, his traits, and his characteristics, she began to find things she genuinely admired and appreciated about him. Writing them down as they occurred to her helped her remember them and reflect on their value. It didn't take long before she could express her honest admiration for some of her husband's strengths.

Of course, finding a few things to admire and appreciate and then learning to express appreciation for them wasn't exactly what Charles needed. He wanted Lori to see the value in him that she had seen when they were dating. So my primary focus of attention was to help Charles give her much more to admire. This required him to do what I've been encouraging throughout this book: meet her top five emotional needs.

You've seen how the Love Bank works, how learning to meet each other's most important emotional needs creates the feeling of love. Well, the process of creating the feelings of admiration and appreciation works in a very similar way. As a husband learns to meet his wife's most important emotional needs, she finds herself responding with a natural and overflowing respect for him. Conversely, if a man does not meet her needs, she cannot in all honesty express the degree of admiration he needs from her. Therefore, much of her admiration depends on his ability to meet her top emotional needs.

With this observation in mind, my plan helps a man identify and meet those needs.

Step 1: Identify Behaviors That Build or Destroy Admiration and Appreciation

I encouraged Lori to make two lists, the first describing behaviors that she admired and appreciated in her husband, the second describing behaviors that destroyed her admiration and appreciation. For both lists, she grouped the behaviors under her top five emotional needs: affection, intimate conversation, financial support, honesty and openness, and family commitment.

This is the list Lori made that described her husband's behaviors.

Behavior That I Admire and Appreciate	Behavior That Destroys My Admiration and Appreciation
Affection	*Affection*
1. Holds my hand when we're out together. 2. Hugs me when he comes home from work. 3. Sends me surprise cards and flowers.	
Intimate Conversation	*Intimate Conversation*
4. Talks to me about how his day went and how I spent mine. 5. Takes an interest in my daily activities and discusses them with me.	1. Buries himself in his work and won't talk to me when I feel upset.
Financial Support	*Financial Support*
	2. Failure to develop his artistic talents 3. Works evenings and weekends 4. Has a career we did not discuss and agree to.
Honesty and Openness	*Honesty and Openness*
6. Always tells me where he has been and leaves numbers where I can reach him in an emergency.	5. Denies something is bothering him even though I can tell he's upset.
Family Commitment	*Family Commitment*
	6. Does not spend enough time with me and our family. 7. Does not discipline the children but leaves the training entirely to me. 8. Rarely shows an interest in our children's activities and never attends PTA meetings.

Lori's list included her disappointment with Charles's choice of a career, which at his stage in life would be very difficult to change. But she also described other disappointments that were almost all related to his failure to meet her need for family commitment. When Lori would become upset with his lack of interest in the children, he would not talk about it. Since he already felt overextended and had no time for the children's projects, he felt that talking about it would not help. So if he were to meet her need for family commitment, their conversation problems as well as their problems with honesty and openness would potentially be overcome.

Step 2: Eliminate Criticism

If Lori had continued to express her issues with Charles in disrespectful ways, there would have been little hope for marital recovery. Her constant criticism of him had driven him away from his family, making any time at home with his family a punishing experience for him. So Lori made a commitment to stop criticizing him about anything. She made her complaints known to him, but they were made without being disrespectful.

The respectful "I would like you to be home with us more often" replaced the disrespectful "You are being a horrible husband and father, and I'm terribly disappointed in you!"

Step 3: Address Behaviors That Destroy Admiration and Appreciation

Then came the toughest part. If Lori was to admire and appreciate Charles, he had to make some major lifestyle changes. Even his career might be at risk because she had not agreed to it. But before addressing his employment, I suggested that they first focus attention on three of Lori's top emotional needs: family commitment, affection, and intimate conversation.

The affectionate and conversational behavior that Lori would have appreciated and admired rarely took place even when Charles was at home. And Charles wasn't home enough to know what Lori might appreciate regarding family commitment. He was an absentee father.

They had come to me for advice. So I gave them the advice that would solve most of their marital problems. But following it wouldn't be easy for them. It would require a complete rearrangement of their schedules. Fortunately, they trusted my judgment and were willing to do whatever I suggested—at least for a while.

First, I wanted Lori and Charles to be in a romantic relationship by spending fifteen hours a week together, giving each other their undivided attention (chap. 2). That would address Lori's emotional needs for affection and intimate conversation, and it would also address the emotional needs that Charles had reported: sexual fulfillment and recreational companionship.

Second, I asked them to spend fifteen hours each week in quality family time. This time would meet Lori's need for family commitment (chap. 11).

That was a total of thirty hours each week that Charles had been spending at work that would now be spent with his family. Could it be done? Could he rearrange his schedule that much right away?

I repeated to Lori and Charles a point I made in chapter 11: couples have the time for both undivided attention and quality family time even when they both have careers. Are a romantic relationship in marriage and quality care of children important enough to make them a priority?

Reminding you what I pointed out in chapter 11, you have 168 hours a week to schedule. I highly recommend 8 hours of sleep each night which leaves you with 112 hours. The time it takes to get ready for work in the morning and ready for bed at night should not take more than another 12 hours. That leaves 100 hours. Your job, including getting there and returning home again, should not take more than 50 hours a week if you want to balance your priorities in life. After carving out time for all of these things, there are still 50 hours left for you to schedule. Fifteen hours for undivided attention and another 15 hours for quality family time leaves you with 20 hours for everything else you want to accomplish: household and childcare tasks, church activities, gardening, hobbies, or just relaxing.

I introduced a weekly schedule to Lori and Charles that I usually suggest to couples with dual careers and small children. It gives undivided attention and quality family time the priority they deserve. Dual careers and small children make the schedule quite challenging, but couples have found that it can be done. After following it for a few weeks, everything falls into place, and they find it to be a very rewarding and productive way to live. The schedule for couples with older children who can care for themselves or one career families with a stay-at-home parent is usually much less challenging.

My plan requires a much tighter schedule than Lori and Charles had been accustomed to having. For one, they had to go to work and return home at about the same time every day. With some creative planning, they could have done that earlier, but they didn't think it was necessary. Also, in the past, their mealtimes had been "every man for himself." My plan required them to have their meals together as a family.

Lori and Charles worked with me to modify my original schedule to fit some of the realities of their lives. But they were able to modify many of their lifestyle habits to conform to my schedule. After making adjustments, this is the schedule we planned together for the first week.

Monday–Friday

6:00—Awake, shower, and dress for both.

6:30—Dress the children together, prepare breakfast together, and eat together as a family (1 hour of quality family time for 5 days equals 5 hours).

7:30—Charles takes the children to childcare and then goes to work. Lori leaves for work.

8:30—Both arrive at work.

8:30 to 4:30—While at work, text or talk to each other by phone at least once in the morning, once at noon, once in the afternoon, and once before leaving work. More often if possible.

4:30—Contact each other to be sure they will arrive home at roughly the same time. Charles leaves work to pick up the children from childcare because his work is closer to home, and Lori leaves work at the same time.

5:00—Charles picks up the children.

Monday, Wednesday, Friday

5:30 to 8:30—Lori and Charles return home, prepare dinner together, have dinner together as a family, clean up the kitchen together, spend the rest of the evening caring for the children, and put them to bed by 8:30 (3 hours of quality family time for 3 days equals 9 hours).

8:30 to 9:30—Complete household tasks together.

9:30 to 10:00—Prepare for bed and go to sleep.

Tuesday and Thursday

5:30 to 6:00—Lori and Charles return home and take the children to Lori's mother's home, where the children will have dinner and be given baths before they are picked up at 9:00. (For some families with smaller children, 9:30 is too late for bedtime, and the schedule must be adjusted to accommodate that reality.)

6:00 to 8:30—Lori and Charles have a date that includes affection, intimate conversation, and recreational companionship. They agree to make love at home (2.5 hours of undivided attention for 2 days equals 5 hours).

8:30 to 9:00—Pick up the children, return home, and put the children to bed.

9:00 to 9:30—Make love (1/2 hour of undivided attention for 2 days equals 1 hour).

9:30 to 10:00—Prepare for bed and go to sleep.

Saturday

6:00 to 8:00—Sleep in if desired, cuddle in bed together when awake, and shower.

8:00 to 9:00—Dress the children together, prepare breakfast together, and eat together as a family (1 hour of quality family time).

9:00 to 10:00—Do domestic chores together so that they are all completed.

10:00 to 3:30—Do any personal projects or activities alone that both agree to. Spend time at work if needed. Watch football or take a nap without being with each other.

3:30 to 4:00—Drop off the children at Lori's mother's home, where they will have dinner and be given baths before they are picked up at 9:00.

4:00 to 9:00—Lori and Charles have a date that includes affection, intimate conversation, and recreational companionship. They make love at home before picking up the children (5 hours of undivided attention).

9:00 to 9:30—Pick up the children, return home, and put the children to bed.

9:30 to 10:00—Prepare for bed and go to sleep.

Sunday

6:00 to 8:00—Sleep in if desired, cuddle in bed together when awake, and shower.

8:00 to 9:00—Dress the children together, prepare breakfast together, and eat together as a family (1 hour of quality family time).

9:00 to 10:00—Get ready to go to church together as a family.

10:00 to 12:00—Attend church together.

12:00 to 5:00—Leave church, have lunch, and visit with all available parents briefly, one at a time, and drop off the children at Lori's mother's home, where they will have dinner and be given baths before they are picked up at 9:00.

5:00 to 9:00—Lori and Charles have a date that includes affection, intimate conversation, and recreational companionship. They make love at home before picking up the children (4 hours of undivided attention).

9:00 to 9:30—Pick up the children, return home, and put the children to bed.

9:30–10:00—Prepare for bed and go to sleep.

Lori's mother was happy to have her grandchildren with her as often as possible, so the fifteen hours she cared for them was easy for Lori and Charles to arrange. But would she be willing to provide that care for years to come? I encouraged Lori and Charles to arrange for alternative caretakers in the case of emergencies, or to take some of the responsibility off of her mother.

In this schedule, 15 hours were planned for undivided attention and 16 hours for quality family time. But to accommodate that change, the hours that Charles was at work had to go from about 75 hours to about 45 hours a week. Could he get the same work done in 45 hours that it had been taking him 75 hours to accomplish? He was a salaried employee, so he wasn't being paid overtime for the extra hours he was at work. He freely admitted, however, that much of the time he had spent at work had been unproductive. So maybe he could be just as productive in fewer hours.

Making Adjustments

After Lori and Charles had completed their first week of dating, I spoke with them by phone while they were on their Tuesday evening date to plan their second week's schedule and make any adjustments they felt were necessary.

The schedule had worked out a lot better than they thought it would. So they left it the way it was. As long as Lori wasn't being critical of Charles, they both enjoyed their time together. In fact, they reported that the schedule lowered their overall level of stress. Their time alone together was their reward for all the other responsibilities they had during the day. It was their way to escape—with each other.

Their childcare and household responsibilities were also more enjoyable. Working together in accomplishing these tasks made Lori particularly happy because she had been somewhat resentful about Charles's lack of participation. She also appreciated knowing when Charles would be arriving at home.

They also enjoyed their careers more than they had before. There was a sparkle in their eyes that others could notice.

After a few weeks, a complete change had taken over Lori. She was in love with Charles again, and she had absolutely no problem praising him for being a great father and lover. Her failure to meet his need for admiration and appreciation was now a thing of the past, and he was in love with her again too. My test for romantic love that I gave them each week, the Love Bank Inventory, confirmed what was so obviously apparent to anyone who saw them together.

Lori's original vision of Charles as an artist disappeared. True, she would have been proud of Charles had he cultivated his artistic ability one way or another, but now she was proud of him for being a great father and husband, and she let him know it regularly. His career in advertising didn't bother her at all now that he was spending time with his family and meeting her top emotional needs.

I checked in with Lori and Charles occasionally, and they reported to me that their new dating schedule had revolutionized their lives. The program had worked.

Every couple I counsel to plan for undivided attention and quality family time creates a unique schedule based on their lifestyle constraints. I begin with a standard schedule that they try to incorporate into their daily routine, and then we change it to conform to the realities of their lives. Lori and Charles were among the more difficult couples to schedule because of their dual careers and young children. Schedules for couples with a single career or older children require much fewer adjustments. But some couples are even more challenging due to their lack of childcare options and other obstacles. I've found that even these couples, however, are eventually able to create a lifestyle that enables them to provide the moral and educational development of their children while also maintaining a romantic relationship with each other through undivided attention.

I have written a series of twenty-three articles on how to achieve these objectives regardless of the obstacles couples may face. While the series title Dating the One You Married (see the "Articles" section of www.marriage builders.com) seems to focus primarily on romantic dating, the articles assume that quality family time is equally important.

What's Next?

Lori had no problem expressing her admiration and appreciation to Charles after he began meeting her top emotional needs. However, some people do not find it easy to express what they are feeling from their heart. Just because they *feel* pride does not mean they communicate it. When that is the case, I encourage an admiring and appreciative spouse to learn how to speak those words of praise, just as they learned any other habit.

First, they have to make an effort to say what they are thinking and feeling, and they have to say it repeatedly. At first, doing so seems awkward, as any new behavior is. But as the habit develops, it becomes smoother and more spontaneous. Eventually, they almost effortlessly express the admiration and appreciation they feel, thereby meeting their spouse's emotional need.

QUESTIONS FOR HER

1. Has the expression of admiration and appreciation toward your husband been a special problem for you? Has he ever asked you to be less critical of him or encouraged you to count your blessings? Are you willing to avoid being critical of him?

2. Do you have the need for admiration and appreciation? How have you tried to communicate that to your husband? How has he responded?

3. Make a list of changes in your husband that would make you a more admiring wife. Divide the list into behaviors that you admire and appreciate and behaviors that destroy your admiration and appreciation. If your husband were to make a similar list of changes that would make him admire and appreciate you more, how would you react? Would you be offended, or would you want to make those changes to help meet his need for admiration and appreciation?

4. What do you think of the schedule that Lori and Charles created to meet each other's intimate emotional needs and Lori's need for family commitment? Is having a romantic relationship and quality family time important enough to you for you to rearrange your schedule?

QUESTIONS FOR HIM

1. Has the expression of admiration and appreciation toward your wife been a special problem for you? Has she ever asked you to be

less critical of her or encouraged you to count your blessings? Are you willing to avoid being critical of her?

2. Do you have the need for admiration and appreciation? How have you tried to communicate that to your wife? How has she responded?

3. Make a list of changes in your wife that would make you a more admiring husband. Divide the list into behaviors that you admire and appreciate and behaviors that destroy your admiration and appreciation. If your wife were to make a similar list of changes that would make her admire and appreciate you more, how would you react? Would you be offended, or would you want to make those changes to help meet her need for admiration and appreciation?

4. What do you think of the schedule that Lori and Charles created to meet each other's intimate emotional needs and Lori's need for family commitment? Is having a romantic relationship and quality family time important enough to you for you to rearrange your schedule?

TO CONSIDER TOGETHER

1. What do you think of the overall plan suggested in this chapter?

2. Are you both willing to avoid criticizing each other?

3. Are you both willing to make a list of changes that would make you more admiring and appreciative of each other?

4. Are you willing to try using a weekly schedule of romantic dating and quality family time like Charles and Lori used?

5. Are you willing to practice admiring and appreciating each other?

THIRTEEN

Protect Your Love Bank from Outside Threats

The feeling of romantic love is extremely important in marriage. It not only provides the passion that you expect from each other but also helps make you eager to meet each other's emotional needs. Everything I've been advising you to do in your marriage is much easier when you're in love. The feeling of love makes these actions seem almost instinctive.

But if you fall in love with someone else, all those instincts that should be directed toward your spouse become directed toward someone else. The rational bond between two people who have committed themselves to care for each other throughout life is replaced by an irrational bond with someone who cannot possibly provide long-term happiness and security. Romantic love in marriage supports the sensible goal of marital security; romantic love outside of marriage ruins everything a family values.

I call the reasoning power of those having an affair "The Fog." They seem incapable of understanding the seriousness of their mistake and the suffering they are causing themselves and others. Romantic love can do that to you. In marriage, romantic love aids our intelligence and helps us achieve some of our most valuable objectives. Outside of marriage, it turns us into fools.

With the risk of falling in love with someone other than your spouse in mind, it's imperative that you guard your Love Bank from outside intruders.

The feeling of love is triggered when someone of the opposite sex has deposited enough love units in your Love Bank to breach the romantic love threshold. "How can someone do that?" you may ask. By now you should know the answer. All that's required is that the person meet one or more of your five most important emotional needs with the quality and quantity to breach the romantic love threshold. If you give someone other than your spouse the opportunity to make you particularly happy and fulfilled, you'll find yourself in The Fog. Everything in you will encourage you to spend more time with this person who makes you feel so good, even if doing so is a threat to your spouse, your children, your values, your livelihood, your health, and everything else important to you.

At the time of your wedding, you and your spouse probably vowed to be faithful to each other—to have an exclusive sexual relationship. But most affairs do not begin with sex. They begin when other important emotional needs are met that trigger romantic love—and that usually leads to sex. Anything someone does that can trigger your feeling of love for them is a danger to your marriage.

So to avoid finding yourself in love with someone other than your spouse, you must guard your Love Bank. You must also be cautious about how you affect the Love Banks of others outside of your marriage.

Before I introduce some important precautions, I need to ask an important question.

Who Is Responsible for an Affair?

I have been counseling couples for over fifty years. Based on my experience with thousands of cases of infidelity, research I have conducted, and studies I have read, I have come to believe that over 60 percent of marriages experience the betrayal of infidelity.

That's a lot of broken promises and commitments. Before you think that it won't happen to you, consider that almost every couple I've worked with was thinking the same thing before it happened.

When helping a couple through the pain of infidelity, I make it clear from the outset that the unfaithful spouse is entirely responsible for the betrayal. I make it simple: no one makes you have an affair. No one.

There may be reasons for having an affair, but those reasons don't change who is responsible. There may be contributing factors that all came together as a perfect storm leading to lines being crossed, but the responsibility doesn't change. Even when an affair develops unintentionally, the unfaithful spouse is responsible for the suffering of the betrayal.

Why should an affair be avoided at all costs? Because it is the most painful betrayal that can occur in marriage, and in life, according to those who have had personal experience. The suffering that an affair causes a betrayed spouse makes the pleasure experienced by the unfaithful spouse pale in comparison.

An affair is preventable. But preventing something from happening depends on having an accurate understanding of who is responsible for preventing it. Any misunderstanding of responsibility creates a reasonable concern for its future occurrence.

Successful recovery after an affair is also dependent on an understanding of who is responsible. Without that understanding, it's unlikely that recovery will take place and likely that an affair will happen again. While the cooperation of both spouses is required for recovery, both must understand that it is the unfaithful spouse who is responsible for the affair.

I will focus attention on prevention in this chapter and on recovery in the next chapter.

Seven Precautions to Protect Your Love Bank from Outside Threats

Since infidelity causes so much pain and misery in marriage, yet is so common, every spouse should be aware of the risk of an affair—the worst thing they could ever do to the one that they promised to love and protect. I've found that there are precautions that prevent infidelity. I've followed them myself throughout my marriage, and I recommend them to everyone I counsel.

1. Affection is the symbolic expression of care and is a powerful emotional need, especially for women. When a man communicates his concern for

the problems a woman faces and his willingness to be there for her when she needs him, he can make such massive Love Bank deposits that she can fall in love with him. Hugs, cards, gifts, and other gestures of kindness that are not intended to trigger romantic feelings can innocently do just that when offered. Wives can make the same mistake when they show affection to other men.

Does this mean that spouses should never hug anyone of the opposite sex? Does it mean that they shouldn't ever help someone of the opposite sex who is in need? I'm not recommending that. What I am recommending is that affection and acts of care to those of the opposite sex should be limited.

One way to determine how limited they should be is for spouses to ask each other how they feel about the way they express affection to others. If one spouse is uncomfortable with the other spouse's affection toward others in general or toward a specific person, they should avoid doing it. Not only is it the thoughtful thing to do, but it can also help couples avoid conditions that may lead to an affair. When a spouse complains that the other spouse's affectionate nature can send the wrong message, they're usually right.

A spouse should not only avoid being affectionate with those of the opposite sex but also resist receiving affection from others. When someone of the opposite sex communicates their willingness to come to the rescue whenever needed, red flags should be waving. Granted, when a spouse's marriage is in trouble, expressions of care can be very uplifting. It's good to know someone cares when your spouse doesn't seem to show much interest. But at this time of vulnerability, you should get help from a trusted advisor or a professional marriage counselor who can provide a solution to your marital problems.

2. Affection and intimate conversation have a great deal in common: they both communicate caring love. That's what makes both of them intimate emotional needs.

Intimate conversation includes personal topics such as your hopes and dreams, the struggles you have in life, your victories and defeats—whatever it is that expresses your deepest thoughts and feelings. Such conversation is very important to almost everyone, but especially to women. When women exchange intimate details of their lives with someone of the opposite sex, massive Love Bank deposits are made. That's why intimate conversation is an essential ingredient in marriage.

But what if the husband refuses to talk? Where does the wife go to relieve her craving for intimate conversation? When a male friend asks the innocent question "How are you feeling?" it's so easy to answer the question honestly. And that intimate conversation would be so fulfilling that she'd likely fall in love with the man who is truly interested in knowing the answer.

Most affairs begin with intimate conversation without any romantic intentions. But the Love Bank doesn't consider intent—it considers only a person's account balance. Once it breaches the romantic love threshold, it triggers romantic love for the wrong person. And that's a tragic outcome for a marriage.

This precaution is especially true for topics about marital problems. When the question "How are you feeling?" is answered with a flood of tears and an expression of deep disappointment in marriage, the other person is highly motivated to come to the rescue: "I'll be there to help when your husband neglects you or treats you badly." A willingness to accept that emotional help is how many affairs begin.

Social networks are one of the most common breeding grounds for infidelity. It makes sense because through these networks people exchange intimate details about themselves and receive support from each other for the problems they face. It's no wonder that so many men and women fall in love with a friend they know only through a social network. So it isn't only face-to-face conversations that should be guarded. All correspondence that reveals your personal problems to someone of the opposite sex should be avoided.

3. Almost all couples begin their marriage with a vow to be sexually faithful. They understand the risks of infidelity. But they don't necessarily understand how exclusive their sex life should be. So I'll repeat a rule to live by that I introduced to you in chapter 5, "Sexual Fulfillment." It maximizes the sexual pleasure they provide each other and minimizes the risk of an affair. I call it the Policy of Sexual Exclusivity: *never engage in any sexual act or experience that does not include your spouse.*

This policy, which limits all forms of sex to marriage, is based on what psychologists call the "contrast effect": when comparing two experiences, the most enjoyable one will make the other one seem boring. So when a spouse tells me that sex has become boring, I suspect competing forms of sex. Pornography, strip clubs, masturbation, and other forms of nonmarital sex are often the culprit. If you want marital sex to be the most enjoyable, it should not compete with other sexual experiences.

But sexual exclusivity requires sexual cooperation. If you are each other's exclusive sex partners, you should provide the quality and quantity of sex that leaves neither of you frustrated. Granted, if you are not in love and have a lower need for sexual fulfillment, this may be a particularly difficult assignment. As with all emotional needs, however, if you engage in lovemaking in as mutually enjoyable a way as possible, Love Bank deposits will be made in the accounts of both spouses. Eventually, when you have restored your love for each other, lovemaking will become almost instinctive.

4. Spend most of your recreational time with your spouse so that when you are having a good time, your spouse is right there enjoying it with you. Avoid recreational activities with someone of the opposite sex who could build a Love Bank balance simply by being with you when you're having fun.

I have found that exercising together can be one of the fastest ways to build Love Bank balances in marriage. There are a host of physiological reasons why so many love units are deposited during a workout. So for that same reason, you should avoid exercising with someone of the opposite sex who is not your spouse. The gym is a very common place for affairs to begin.

5. If someone of the opposite sex ever tells you they find you attractive, thank that person for the compliment but don't return it. Also, tell your spouse about the compliment. In general, avoid telling anyone of the opposite sex, other than your spouse, that you feel they are attractive. If your feelings of attraction are ever revealed, avoid seeing or talking to that person.

6. Avoid contact with all past lovers. High school and college reunions, weddings, and even funerals are notorious places for breaking this precaution. If one of these events must be attended, have your spouse by your side at all times.

7. Even if you take all the precautions I've recommended, and others besides, it's possible for someone to make enough Love Bank deposits to breach your romantic love threshold. If you ever find yourself infatuated with someone other than your spouse, for whatever reasons, don't walk away—run! Avoid that person at all costs.

If that ever happens to you, the first person to know about it should be your spouse. Then plan with your spouse how you will break off contact with that person. It's often a friend or even a relative of your spouse who has the opportunity to make that many Love Bank deposits, and breaking off contact with that person is not easy to do. I can't tell you how many "best friends" of a spouse have turned out to be the betrayer. But it makes sense that a friend or relative would be in the best position to make Love Bank deposits. Regardless of who it is, have nothing to do with them, even if it means quitting your job, leaving your church, or moving from your neighborhood. And above all, don't ever tell them how you feel.

These precautions are meant to be driven with a sense of personal responsibility: "It's up to me to guard my emotional needs." Avoid allowing yourself to believe that your spouse is in any way responsible for protecting your Love Bank from other people. Never threaten, or even suggest, that if your needs are not met, you will be forced to go elsewhere to have them met. Instead, continue to use this book, and others I've written, to learn with your spouse how to provide for each other with mutual enjoyment.

As I mentioned before, I've followed these precautions I've listed throughout my entire married life, and I don't feel the least bit constrained or unhappy. They've helped me avoid an affair, the worst thing I could have ever done to my wife, Joyce. That's certainly worth every precaution I've taken. It's like avoiding anything that creates a high risk—like smoking. Why raise the risk of lung or throat cancer? Whatever immediate pleasure a person might experience doesn't compare to the long, slow death that many chronic smokers are forced to endure.

Those who have not followed these precautions until after they've had an affair usually realize their value and wish they had followed them sooner. But those who fail to see their value and are unwilling to take these precautions will continue to be at risk for future pain and loss.

These suggestions are only a minor inconvenience when compared to the disaster of infidelity. And they do more than prevent an affair—they also build a stronger emotional bond in the marriage. They're well worth taking.

Checklist to Make Love Bank Deposits

Part I: Meet the Most Important Emotional Needs

1. Identify your most important emotional needs:

   - ○ Read about the ten most important emotional needs in appendix A.
   - ○ Make two copies of the Emotional Needs Questionnaire in appendix B, one for you and one for your spouse.
   - ○ Complete the questionnaire and rank your top five emotional needs according to their importance.

2. Become an expert at meeting your spouse's most important emotional needs:

   - ○ Agree to become an expert at meeting each other's top five emotional needs.
   - ○ Discover how to meet each other's emotional needs regarding quantity and quality ("How often would you like me to meet that need?" and "How would you like me to meet that need?").
   - ○ When giving feedback on quality and quantity, offer specific and positive suggestions ("I'd love it if you would do ___.") instead of only negative feedback.
   - ○ Allow time for a new behavior that meets an emotional need to become comfortable and then enjoyable.
   - ○ Meet each other's needs in ways that are mutually enjoyable. Never expect your spouse to suffer.
   - ○ Continue to give each other feedback regarding your most important emotional needs. Regularly schedule a time for feedback until both of you are meeting each other's needs.
   - ○ Read *His Needs, Her Needs* and use its accompanying workbook, *Five Steps to Romantic Love*, if you need help learning how to become an expert at meeting your spouse's most important emotional needs.

Part II: Take Time for Undivided Attention

Follow the Policy of Undivided Attention:

1. Privacy
   - Plan your time together to be without children, relatives, or friends.
   - Avoid other distractions so that you can give each other your undivided attention.

2. Objectives
   - Choose activities that will meet the emotional needs of affection, sexual fulfillment, intimate conversation, and recreational companionship when you schedule your time together.
   - Choose recreational activities that are mutually enjoyable.

3. Amount
   - Schedule at least fifteen hours for undivided attention each week. Choose a time each week to make that schedule.
   - Overcome financial obstacles that prevent giving each other undivided attention:
     - Join or start a babysitting co-op.
     - Rearrange your budget priorities.
     - Be creative and choose inexpensive recreational activities.
   - Try to schedule your dates for the same time every week.

Part III: Protect Your Love Bank from Outside Threats

- Avoid meeting the important emotional needs of someone of the opposite sex who is not your spouse and avoid having your needs met by someone of the opposite sex who is not your spouse, with special emphasis on affection, sexual fulfillment, intimate conversation, and recreational companionship.
- Avoid contact with past lovers.
- If you ever find yourself infatuated with someone other than your spouse, for whatever reasons, don't walk away—run! And tell your spouse.

FOURTEEN

How to Survive an Affair

If both you and your spouse follow the advice I've given you in this book, especially the advice I gave you in the last chapter, you will never need to know how to survive an affair because you will never have that dreaded experience. But if an affair has taken place in your marriage, this chapter will help guide you from disaster to safety.

At first, I didn't think that marriages could survive an affair. I didn't know of any that had survived. But couples I counseled kept wanting me to help them recover, usually for the sake of their children. So, over time, I was able to put together a plan for recovery that addressed just about every issue and complication that occurred. This chapter is a brief summary of that very successful plan. The complete plan can be found in my book *Surviving an Affair*.

The Anatomy of an Affair

Alex sighed quietly as he reached over to turn out the light. Then he turned back to kiss Jasmine's cheek. "Good night, honey," he whispered.

No answer. Jasmine was sound asleep. That did not surprise him, and he knew how angry she'd be if he woke her just to make love. He lay down and pulled the covers over his shoulder. Long ago he had given up the loser's game of feeling sorry for himself. He just had to face the fact that Jasmine no longer had any interest in sex. She used to, he'd thought, in the early years of their marriage, before the children came along.

The next morning as Alex caught the 7:30 commuter train, he greeted Heather and Brandon, who also worked for his firm. As Alex scrolled through the morning news on his phone, he remembered his open lunch schedule.

"Hey, you two," he called out. "My lunch partner's out of town today. Either of you free?"

"Sorry," Brandon told him, "I have to be across town."

Alex looked at Heather, a tall, willowy woman, studious and plain. "I'd love to go to lunch with you," she answered brightly.

I haven't seen her in a while, Alex thought. Heather had gone to his high school, and they'd lost track of each other for a few years until they started working for the same company. Their friendship had been rekindled several months before when they began working on the same team to install a new computer system. Once they'd completed that, though, Alex's responsibilities had taken him to the fifth floor, while she had stayed on the seventh.

"You know," Alex told her that day at lunch, "I'm kind of glad Brandon had to go across town today."

"Me too," she agreed, smiling. "I've missed you since you went downstairs. We should have done this sooner."

"Yeah. Working on that project was the most fun I've had in a long time."

"The system's really proving itself too. Float time on orders has been reduced to almost nothing."

"That doesn't surprise me." Alex chuckled. "Why, with you and me on that job, it *couldn't* fail."

As they left the restaurant, Alex and Heather made plans to meet again the next week. Soon the midweek lunch date had become a regular part of their schedules. Once, Heather gave Alex a book on cryptocurrencies, and a few weeks later he responded with a modest but lovely bracelet. As he gave it to her at lunch, her face lit up. Leaning over the table, she kissed him gently on the cheek.

"Heather, I have to be honest," he told her awkwardly. "I'm getting awfully attached to you. It's . . . well, it's more than friendship."

"Alex," she responded, her voice low, "I feel that way too."

"I've never told you how I feel about Jasmine . . ."

"And you never need to," she reassured him.

"But I want to. I've never been able to talk to anyone about it before. I'd like to now."

"Then go ahead. It's okay."

"When I married her, I didn't realize what I was getting myself into. I thought we shared a lot of interests, would spend a lot of time together, but all that dried up within a year or so. Now she does her thing, and I do mine. She doesn't like me to talk to her about work, and she complains I don't earn enough money. Half the time, when I get home at night, it's like walking into a madhouse."

Heather listened in sympathetic silence. After work, he stopped by her place "to talk."

The next morning when Alex woke up in Heather's bed, he thought how pretty she looked. He kissed her bare shoulder and smiled as she opened her eyes. "Hi, handsome," she whispered.

"Hello, beautiful."

After that evening, Alex and Heather seemed obsessed with each other. Never in his life had Alex experienced such enthusiastic and consistent lovemaking.

At first, Jasmine had only some vague doubts about Alex, but soon her doubts turned to suspicions as his absences increased. In addition to the occasional stay in town overnight, he started leaving the house on weekend afternoons. Finally, one night she decided to test her suspicions and called Jake, with whom Alex said he planned to spend the night. Jake tried to say Alex hadn't arrived yet, but his hesitation left Jasmine unconvinced. When she tried to call Alex, he didn't answer the phone.

Jasmine remembered hearing Alex talk warmly about working with Heather on a computer project. She also knew Heather didn't live too far away and decided she might be a likely prospect. One Saturday afternoon after Alex had disappeared, Jasmine hired a neighborhood teenager to watch the children and drove to Heather's apartment. As soon as she turned onto her block, she spotted Alex's car parked just around the corner.

Jasmine parked, found Heather's apartment, and took a deep breath as she rang the bell. Heather answered the door wearing a nightgown. "Jasmine!" she said just a bit too loudly. "Why, what a surprise . . ."

"I'm sorry, Heather, if this seems rude, but I must come in to see something for myself." She brushed past the other woman and walked through the apartment into the bedroom. There she found Alex hurriedly pulling on his pants. The rest of his clothes were still draped over a chair near the bed.

"Jasmine! I—"

Jasmine spun around and walked out of the apartment without saying a word. She saw no signs of Heather and didn't even bother to close the door on her way out. Once in her car, Jasmine burst into tears. As she drove home, she attempted to force her numb mind to think. Divorce seemed her only option.

Alex and Heather stood by the front window and watched Jasmine drive away. "What will you do?" Heather asked.

"I have to go after her and try to cool her down. Don't worry about it, love. It's going to work out."

When he got home, Alex saw Jasmine's car, engine running and door ajar, standing in the driveway. He turned off the ignition, pocketed the key, and closed the door. As he walked through the front door, he heard the children crying. The bewildered babysitter told him his wife had gone upstairs. He paid her and sent her home, then went to find Jasmine. She had locked herself in the bedroom. After calling to her a few times, he realized he'd better take care of the kids first. They went out for some fast food, and he put them to bed. All that time the door to the bedroom remained tightly shut.

Again, Alex knocked on the door. No answer. "Jasmine, please," he begged softly.

The lock on the knob clicked, and he tried the door again. As it opened, he saw Jasmine sitting on the bed, eyes swollen from crying. He walked over to her. "I'm so ashamed, honey—"

"Don't you *dare* call me honey!" she hissed.

"But, Jasmine, I love you and the children. You mean the world to me. I don't understand how I could have done this to you." Again, Jasmine started sobbing, and instinctively Alex tried to comfort her.

"Don't touch me!" she gasped, struggling away from him to perch in the middle of the bed. "How could you do that? I hate the sight of you!"

"Jasmine, please. . . . It'll never happen again. I must have been crazy. Please give me another chance." Tears welled up in his eyes.

"You liar! You lied to me about all those nights you had to spend at Jake's, didn't you?!"

"Jasmine, please, no—"

"Don't lie. It only makes it worse!"

"You're right, and I won't lie anymore. You have to believe me! I can only promise you it won't happen again. You and the kids mean too much to me. It's all over, Jasmine. I mean it."

This sort of exchange continued until three o'clock in the morning—Alex begging Jasmine for mercy and understanding, and Jasmine ripping into him with rage and anguish. Finally, driven by exhaustion, she permitted a truce and allowed Alex to come to bed with her.

During the next few days, Alex continued to show remorse and managed to quiet Jasmine down somewhat. By the end of the week, he had her convinced that temporary insanity had caused his fling with Heather and that it wouldn't happen again.

Alex did stop seeing Heather for lunch, but he called her at the first opportunity. "I have to see you, but I don't dare right now. I love you so much—I just don't know what to do."

"Alex, I love you too. There'll never be any question of that. But I want you to hold your marriage together. I don't want to cause a divorce."

"Heather, you're a jewel. Don't worry. I'll give it my best shot. If it ends in divorce, it won't be your fault."

Alex held out for two weeks and then rendezvoused with Heather for lunch at an out-of-the-way spot. "I can't stop thinking about you and what we have together. I've never had anything like it in my life, and I know I won't ever have it again."

Heather could only hold Alex's hand and weep. The next week they met at Jake's apartment and resumed the affair with renewed vigor. It seemed as if they had new energy, stored up over the past weeks of separation. After that, they got together whenever possible. Staying in town overnight was out because Jasmine would suspect. One Saturday afternoon, however, Alex couldn't stand it and quietly left for Heather's apartment. He didn't realize that Jasmine had seen him go and had followed. They repeated the whole sorry discovery scene, which left Jasmine utterly inconsolable. She ordered Alex out of the house and filed for divorce.

Alex thought about moving in with Heather but decided against it. Instead, he found a room to rent, where he sat and thought about what had happened. He realized not only that he missed Jasmine and the children but also that he had many other things to think about—being rejected by his family and friends and having to spend large sums of money on lawyers, alimony, and child support. He also thought about his company and their policy concerning affairs and keeping families together. He could lose his job—or at least miss an upcoming promotion.

One evening, about a week after he had moved out, Alex phoned Jasmine. "Please give me one more chance. I think our marriage was in trouble long before this thing happened. I know there were things I was trying to ignore, and I was wrong to do that. I should have brought it all out in the open with you and a counselor. Jasmine, I really want to save our marriage and our family. Will you go to see someone with me?"

At first, Jasmine didn't know how to reply. Was Alex right? Maybe she was partly to blame. And he did want to see a counselor.

"Okay," she finally responded. "I'll give it a try."

Before the week was out, Alex had moved back home. He managed one brief conversation with Heather, telling her he still loved her but that he could not get a divorce—not yet, anyway.

During counseling sessions, Alex tried to explain his feelings about why he felt the marriage had gone wrong—and why he held resentment against Jasmine.

"Alex," said the counselor, "you need to spell out what you thought was wrong. Let's get specific."

Alex got specific and talked about Jasmine's indifference to having sex, her lack of interest in his career, and her unwillingness to share in activities he enjoyed. Then he cited the incessant nagging about household problems, even though she had never had to go out and get a job.

As Jasmine listened, she began to wonder if perhaps a lot of the problem was really her fault.

Then the counselor zeroed in and asked Alex to be totally honest. Was he still in love with Heather?

"Yes, I am," Alex said with a mixture of shame and defiance. Alex didn't bother to say that he and Heather had resumed their affair and still spent lunch hours at Jake's apartment. The counselor did not ask.

In the following months, Alex managed to remain in counseling while continuing his affair with Heather. He fooled both Jasmine and the counselor into believing he was interested in being permanently faithful to his wife. He learned how to be more careful and less impulsive in his frequent meetings with Heather.

Alex, Jasmine, and Heather are caught in the proverbial love triangle, and it's not going to end well unless they take steps that will seem counterintuitive to them at first. As I explained in the last chapter, the responsibility of the affair should lie squarely with Alex. Yet, Jasmine is thinking that it might have been her fault, and their counselor is doing nothing to counter that impression. Alex is able to fool both the counselor and Jasmine by focusing their attention on her rather than on him.

Couples come to me with their versions of how something so shocking and painful could have happened to them. And each time I must help them understand the real reason: Alex failed to guard his Love Bank. It's that understanding that helps me set into motion a plan that will address the trauma they feel, help them avoid the risk of another affair, create transparency in their relationship, and restore their romantic relationship.

Steps to Surviving an Affair

Often, people ask, "How do you help people like Alex and Jasmine survive an affair? What do you tell a couple when this actually happens to them?"

Frankly, when I first started counseling couples caught in the snare of infidelity, I didn't think their marriages could survive. At best, I thought they might stick it out for the sake of their children and live a life of resentment and regret. I had no idea they could survive the ordeal and create a better marriage than they had ever experienced.

As it turns out, I've discovered that really the only way to survive an affair is for a couple to follow my rules of recovery, which will turn their marriage into a passionate and fulfilling experience. Unless they have a better marriage than ever before, spouses don't stay together.

My plan to achieve this remarkable result takes a couple down a very narrow path. There are plenty of rules to follow, and without the complete cooperation of both spouses, it won't work. But when the plan is followed, the results are outstanding, and there are thousands of happy couples who bear witness to the plan's amazing rate of success.

A more complete description of this plan is provided in my book *Surviving an Affair*. You can also find additional information on the website www.marriagebuilders.com.

You may need guidance if either you or your spouse is reluctant to follow the plan the way it is presented. As you search for help, consider the Marriage Builders Coaching Center.

Step 1: End the Affair

The first step on the path to surviving an affair is for it to end. An affair ends when the straying spouse ceases all contact with the other person (OP) and never sees or talks to that person again. Time and again I've watched what happens when a drastic and decisive break with the OP is not made. They try to remain "friends" and maintain casual social contact. But inevitably they find their way back into each other's arms. It seems that when it comes to this one person, the spouse exhibits incredibly flawed judgment and an almost irresistible force draws them back.

But even if there is no risk of rekindling the affair, if any contact continues, the affair remains alive in the mind of the betrayed spouse. Since an affair is one of the most hurtful and selfish acts that one spouse can inflict on the other, any contact restores the memory and perpetuates the pain. It's the ultimate betrayal.

For some, the affair ends the right way. The unfaithful spouse sends a letter (see *Surviving an Affair*, Harley and Chalmers) to the lover that communicates how much suffering the affair caused the betrayed spouse and how thoughtless it was; the letter expresses a desire to rebuild the marriage and makes it clear that all contact must be terminated forever. The betrayed spouse reads the letter and approves of it before it's sent. After the letter is sent, extraordinary precautions that I'll explain in the next step are taken to avoid future contact with the lover.

But most affairs end the wrong way—they die a natural death. Instead of taking control of the situation and making a decision to end it, most unfaithful spouses continue in the relationship as long as possible. Affairs, however, don't usually last very long. I estimate that 95 percent of them don't last two years. The few couples who eventually marry have an extremely fragile relationship and are much more likely to divorce than the average couple. So if an affair doesn't end the right way, it will almost always end, even if it's the wrong way.

If your unfaithful spouse is unwilling to end the affair the right way, I know of a way to help speed up its demise: expose it. Your family should know—your parents, your siblings, and even your children. The family of your spouse's lover should also know, especially the OP's spouse. The pastor of your church should be informed as well. Exposure of an affair is like opening a moldy closet to the light of day. Affairs do well when they're conducted in secret, but when they're in full view for all to see, they appear as they are—incredibly foolish and thoughtless.

Even if exposure was ineffective in ending an affair, I'd recommend it anyway. The betrayed spouse needs as much support as possible, and exposure helps friends and relatives understand what's going on. Keeping an affair secret is no real help to anyone, and I've been amazed at how well exposing an affair dismantles the illusion that it rests on. Instead of assuming that the relationship is made in heaven, an unfaithful spouse quickly senses that it's a one-way ticket to hell on earth.

The first reaction of an unfaithful spouse to exposure is to try to turn the tables on the betrayed spouse. "I will never be able to forgive you for hurting me this way. Didn't you think about how I'd be affected by this?" Of course, it's really the affair that hurts. The exposure simply identifies the source of the pain. The unfaithful spouse should be the one begging for forgiveness.

In spite of the suffering that an affair inflicts on a betrayed spouse, during this period of exposure, they should try to make as many Love Bank deposits as they are willing to make and as few withdrawals as possible. If you argue about the affair, you'll damage recovery. Insist on the unfaithful spouse's complete separation from the lover (no contact for life) but don't fight about it. I call this strategy to end the affair Plan A.

If exposure doesn't end the affair immediately, my advice regarding what to do next is different for husbands and wives. I encourage most husbands to try to stick to avoiding arguments and to meet their unfaithful wife's emotional needs (Plan A) as long as possible (six months to a year). But I encourage most wives to separate after about three weeks if their husband is still in contact with his lover. My experience has taught me that the health of most women deteriorates quickly and significantly while living with an unfaithful husband. Men, on the other hand, tend to be able to weather the storm longer with fewer emotional or physical effects. I call the strategy of a complete separation Plan B (see *Surviving an Affair* for more information on Plan A and Plan B).

In addition to avoiding health problems, a separation also helps keep the unfaithful spouse's account in the betrayed spouse's Love Bank from dwindling any further. Daily interaction with an unfaithful spouse causes such large withdrawals that a separation with no contact between spouses can actually help the marriage by temporarily freezing the betrayed spouse's Love Bank. When the affair is over, the betrayed spouse is less likely to divorce when the unfaithful spouse wants to give the marriage a chance to recover.

Yet another advantage to separation is that some of the emotional needs met by the betrayed spouse are suddenly no longer being met. This is especially true when a couple has children. Often, an unfaithful spouse overlooks the betrayed spouse's contribution to the family. While the OP may meet two emotional needs that were unmet by the betrayed spouse, the betrayed spouse may have been meeting the other three that cannot be easily met by the OP. During a separation, the unfaithful spouse can become acutely aware of what is missing.

When a betrayed spouse decides that it's time to separate, I recommend complete separation with absolutely no direct contact (Plan B). The unfaithful spouse should be given the choice of having contact with the betrayed spouse or the OP, but not both. Someone should be appointed to go between the spouses, delivering messages and children during visitation. But until the unfaithful spouse promises to completely end the affair, with absolutely no contact with the lover, the separation should continue. After the separation has lasted two years, with the unfaithful spouse's contact with the lover continuing, I generally recommend a divorce.

Step 2: Create Transparency

When a wayward spouse ends the affair and agrees to rebuild the marriage, extraordinary precautions must be taken to guarantee that there will be no relapses. Affairs thrive on what I've called a *secret second life*. It's what you do under the radar. You know, or at least suspect, that your spouse wouldn't approve, so a part of your life is hidden from them. When a spouse is able to come and go without any accountability, they, like Alex, can have an affair with relative impunity. The temptation of an affair is great because there's little to stop it.

So I encourage spouses to end their secret second lives by being *transparent* in the way they live their lives. This not only guards against affairs but also helps create intimacy and build compatibility. Transparency is not a punishment for bad behavior—it's an essential ingredient for a healthy marriage.

Transparency occurs when couples follow the Policy of Radical Honesty that I introduced in chapter 7: "Reveal to your spouse as much information about yourself as you know—your thoughts, feelings, habits, likes, dislikes, past history, daily activities, and future plans."

Location apps are a great tool for transparency. But the wayward spouse must understand that such an app is not to be seen as a tool for the betrayed spouse to become a probation officer. Instead, it is to be used as a way of being thoughtful and considerate of the fact that the betrayed spouse is struggling to reestablish faith in their spouse. Information about where you are is extremely helpful in trying to rebuild trust. To be seen as trustworthy, you must establish a trustworthy track record. A location app is just the ticket for that.

Also, nothing should be hidden. Passwords, email, text messages, telephone logs, computer histories, and all other forms of communication must be readily available to a spouse. It's the way my wife, Joyce, and I have lived during our fifty-eight years of marriage. By revealing everything we know about ourselves, we have avoided an affair, and our transparency has helped our marriage in a host of other ways too. It's not a lifetime prison sentence in which disclosure prevents us from having what we need most—it's the formula for a very fulfilling life.

If I were to counsel Alex, I would encourage him to give Jasmine a twenty-four-hour-a-day schedule of his whereabouts, and Jasmine should do the same. They would not be acting as probation officers but rather as spouses who want to maintain an emotional connection. Such a schedule is essential in a great marriage because spouses who are partners in life check with each other throughout the day to coordinate their decisions and activities. Jasmine should call him several times a day, and he should call her as well, just so they can check in with each other.

How does this twenty-four-hour-a-day checking in feel? Admittedly, there is one real drawback to this kind of checkup system for someone like Alex. While it will provide Jasmine some reassurance, it is likely to be very annoying to Alex, at least in the beginning. Being accustomed to an independent lifestyle, he must now account for his time and activities. He must consider Jasmine's feelings whenever he does anything. In other words, he is forced to be thoughtful and considerate to his wife. That's what couples do in successful marriages, but Alex hasn't relearned to be thoughtful and considerate when he makes decisions, and, at first, he will feel as if he's married to a parole officer.

Typically, an unfaithful spouse, confronted with the demands of transparency and having no contact with his former OP, responds with depression. Alex may be trying to save his marriage, but he feels miserable. Now cut off from Heather—somebody he loves very much and who met some of his most important emotional needs—and with the checkup going, he feels trapped.

Step 3: Meet Each Other's Emotional Needs

In an affair, the most important emotional needs are usually met: affection, intimate conversation, sexual fulfillment, and recreational companionship. When the decision is finally made to reconcile and to avoid all contact with the OP, it's usually with the hope that the betrayed spouse can learn to meet those emotional needs. I've found that they are met for most of the couples I've counseled.

But the betrayed spouse can do more than the OP could ever do, especially if the couple has children. The OP will simply never be able to take the place of the spouse in the family, but the spouse *can* take the place of the OP.

I've capitalized on this advantage for most of the years I've counseled couples. My question to the unfaithful spouse is, "If you were in love with your spouse, who would you choose to spend the rest of your life with?"

The typical response is "But I'm not in love with my spouse." When I repeat the question "But if you were in love with your spouse, who would you choose to spend the rest of your life with," the answer is always the spouse. It's the logical answer because of all the advantages to the family in keeping the marriage together.

So my primary goal in helping couples recover after an affair is for them to establish a romantic relationship that's just as passionate as the affair. I don't want their choice to be between passion and reason—the affair offering passion and the marriage offering reason. I want them to have passion *and* reason, something that can be found only in their marriage.

If all goes according to my plan, Jasmine will make herself available to Alex sexually and start joining him in some of his favorite activities in a mutually enjoyable way. An ideal scenario would find her reading a book about computers and programming to better understand what he does for a living, and to put icing on the cake, she could start giving him more support at home and stop criticizing him about how he doesn't earn enough money or do enough around the house.

All this could take many weeks or months. Alex probably didn't show Jasmine enough affection or intimate conversation, and that's why she resisted him sexually. Instead of simply judging Jasmine for not being interested in his computer world, he will have to learn how to talk to her about *her* interests and feelings. Jasmine needs very deeply the quality of conversation Alex shared with Heather.

Obviously, Jasmine's emotional need for honesty and openness has fallen into serious disrepair. Alex will have to work long and hard to regain her trust, but he can do it if he learns how to become transparent with her.

I would make a special point to warn Jasmine that she has started down a long and bumpy road. In fact, for a while, she may receive little positive return for her efforts. She should not expect that, as a result of all the changes in her behavior, Alex will suddenly become more loving, caring, and faithful. Rather, as I mentioned, Alex will react initially with depression. If he describes his thoughts honestly, he will tell Jasmine that he spends a great deal of time thinking about Heather. Jasmine could even expect some lying and deceit on Alex's part at first. Alex will feel tempted to try to sneak away to meet Heather again.

Regardless of how well Jasmine meets Alex's needs, he will remain attracted to Heather for some time to come. Even if Jasmine and Alex reignite the flame of their own love by meeting each other's five most important emotional needs, all their efforts may not completely extinguish the flame of attraction ignited by Alex's affair with Heather. It may burn low but never go out completely. Just as an alcoholic remains addicted to alcohol the rest of his life and never dares to touch another drink, Alex will remain vulnerable to Heather for life and should not see her ever again. You are always vulnerable to past romantic relationships.

A Stronger Marriage

A person who discovers their spouse is having an affair experiences one of the most severe blows anyone could possibly sustain. It also sends both partners on an emotional roller coaster. But when a couple follows my narrow path to recovery, they often tell me that they have built a better love relationship than they ever would have had if the affair had not jolted them into constructive action. The affair provides the traumatic trigger that finally gets the spouses to meet each other's important emotional needs. Once they start meeting those basic needs, their marriage becomes what it was supposed to have been all along.

Granted, most people who have never been through recovery after an affair feel that they could never love or trust an unfaithful spouse again. But the thousands of couples I've guided down this narrow path are living proof that this is not true.

It's certainly more difficult to learn to meet each other's emotional needs after an affair than it would have been before an affair. And it's a lot more painful. But with or without an affair, spouses can create a very passionate and fulfilling marriage if they simply learn to meet each other's emotional needs, especially the intimate emotional needs of affection, intimate conversation, sexual fulfillment, and recreational companionship.

FIFTEEN

From Incompatible
to Irresistible

Before I finish this book, I want to draw your attention to two important words: *incompatible* and *irresistible*. Within the definitions of these words lies the key to understanding and applying to your own marriage the insights I have presented. According to *The American Heritage Dictionary*, the definition of *incompatible* is "inharmonious; antagonistic." The definition of *irresistible* is "having an overpowering appeal."

When a husband and a wife can't get along, we may describe them as *incompatible*. Yet at one time, we would have called those same two people *irresistible* to each other. Because they found each other irresistible, they made a lifetime commitment in marriage. Couples start out irresistible and only become incompatible as they leave each other's emotional needs unmet. When someone outside of the marriage offers to meet those needs, an affair starts. Then the other person (OP) becomes irresistible.

But saying the OP is irresistible can be misleading. The OP is seldom *totally* irresistible. In most affairs, the OP meets only some—usually one or two—of the emotional needs of the unfaithful spouse. The betrayed spouse still fulfills the other three or four emotional needs. As I've tried to show time and again, when the unfaithful spouse is caught in the web of an affair, they feel a strong need for both people—the spouse left at home and the OP. The thought of losing either of them seems unbearable.

Some people I counsel manage to bite the bullet and make a choice between the two. Some choose the spouse, and some choose the OP. In either case, they move from guilt and shame to grief and pain. They feel and act depressed because the needs once met by the person they chose to leave now go unmet.

For example, when a unfaithful husband chooses to return to his wife, he probably feels that he has made some great sacrifice for his family. In most cases, he has been forced to give up a satisfying sexual relationship—perhaps the first he has ever known in his life. Any good feelings he may derive from "having done the right thing" do little to lessen his pain or cool his resentment at the loss of what he had in the affair.

If this same unfaithful man chooses his OP, he feels nearly overwhelmed by guilt and shame for having abandoned a wife who has loved and cared for him in many ways. If children are involved, the guilt and shame multiply rapidly. A common lie spread on talk shows and in popular books and articles is that divorce doesn't necessarily damage children. Granted, in some exceptional cases, a divorce may be the better of two evils—for example, when a marriage involves severe alcoholism, child (and domestic) abuse, insanity, and so on. But in the vast majority of cases I've witnessed, divorce devastates children. To rationalize otherwise not only ignores the facts, but it's also cruel.

In my experience, the spouse trapped in an affair comes through the experience relatively healthy when they choose to resolve incompatibility at home and rebuild the marriage. But those I have counseled who have abandoned their marriage in favor of the affair suffer relentless guilt. Those few who manage to avoid the natural death of most affairs and marry their OP find the same problems cropping up in their new marriage. If they ever resolve these problems, they usually know they could have done the same thing to save their first marriage.

The Cure for Incompatibility

The quickest cure for incompatibility and the fastest road to becoming irresistible lie in meeting each other's most important emotional needs.

Happily married couples are already aware of this principle and have learned how to make their marriages a full-time priority. These couples invest the *effort*, and they put it in the *right places*.

I have seen this principle work in many different situations. For example, I once managed a dating service in the Twin Cities area. This service was designed to help people with common interests and objectives meet each other. But soon after I opened the service, I began to see a very real problem. Those who had enrolled—some five hundred—needed more than just an opportunity to meet people. Almost without exception, these people lacked skills in meeting the emotional needs of others. Yet each of them eagerly sought someone else who would be highly skilled at meeting *their* needs and who would take care of *them*. They complained that they met only selfish and insensitive people. Of course, they could not see their own selfishness and insensitivity.

So I reorganized the dating service. Rather than help my subscribers meet eligible people, I helped them become eligible people to meet. I helped them develop skills and other qualities that would make them attractive to those of the opposite sex.

A number of the dating-service subscribers bought into my new concept and made the effort to become skillful at meeting the needs of other people. For these men and women, my dating service was a roaring success. Their newly acquired abilities made them attractive to the opposite sex wherever they went. Many of them married within two years.

I believe our society's failure to train people to meet the needs of others—especially the needs of a marriage partner—has played a large part in our high divorce rate. Marriage is not a simple social institution that everyone enters into because eventually they fall in love and live happily ever after. As long as we fail to see marriage as a complex relationship that requires special training and abilities to meet the needs of a member of the opposite sex, we will continue to see a discouraging and devastating divorce rate.

Before I do a quick review of what it takes to be an irresistible man or woman, let me repeat what I wrote in the first chapter of this book: "Every person is unique. While men on average pick five particular emotional needs as their most important and women on average pick the other five, any

individual can pick any combination of the basic ten. Although I have identified the most important emotional needs of the average man and woman,
I don't know the emotional needs of any particular husband or wife. So
it's very important for each couple to complete their own questionnaires
to gain insight into what they can do to make each other the happiest."

This review of what it takes, on average, to be an irresistible man or
woman should be read with the understanding that you and your spouse
can modify it to reflect your unique combination of most important emotional needs.

The Irresistible Man

A husband can make himself irresistible to his wife by learning to meet
her five most important emotional needs, the following being statistically
most common.

1. *Affection.* Her husband tells her that he cares for her with words,
   cards, flowers, gifts, and common courtesies. He hugs and kisses
   her many times each day, creating an environment of affection that
   clearly and repeatedly expresses his care for her.
2. *Intimate conversation.* He sets aside time every day to talk to her.
   They may talk about events in their lives, their children, their feelings, or their plans. But whatever the topic, she enjoys the conversation because it is never demanding, judgmental, or angry but always informative and constructive. She talks to him as much as she
   would like, and he responds with interest. He is never too busy to
   "just talk." The way he talks to her conveys his caring love for her.
3. *Honesty and openness.* He tells her everything about himself, leaving nothing out that might surprise her later. He describes his positive and negative feelings, events of his past, his daily schedule, and
   his plans for the future. He never leaves her with a false impression and is truthful about his thoughts, feelings, intentions, and
   behavior.
4. *Financial support.* He assumes the responsibility to house, feed,
   and clothe the family. If his income is insufficient to provide

essential support, he resolves the problem by upgrading his skills to increase his salary. He does not work long hours, keeping himself from his wife and family, but is able to provide necessary support by working a forty- to fifty-hour week. While he encourages his wife to pursue a career if it is her desire, he does not depend on her salary for family living expenses.

5. *Family commitment*. He commits sufficient time and energy to the moral and educational development of the children. He reads to them, engages in sports with them, and takes them on frequent outings. He reads books and attends lectures with his wife on the subject of child development so they will do a good job training the children. They discuss training methods and objectives until they agree. He does not proceed with any plan of training or discipline without her approval and recognizes that his care of the children is critically important to her.

When a woman finds a man who meets her five most important emotional needs, she will find him irresistible.

The Irresistible Woman

A wife can make herself irresistible to her husband by learning to meet his five most important emotional needs, the following being statistically most common.

1. *Sexual fulfillment*. His wife meets this need by becoming a terrific sexual partner. She studies her own sexual responses to recognize and understand what brings out the best in her; then she shares this information with him, and together they learn to have a sexual relationship that they both find repeatedly satisfying and enjoyable.

2. *Recreational companionship*. She develops an interest in the recreational activities he likes most and tries to become proficient at them. If she finds she cannot enjoy them, she encourages him to consider other activities that they can do together. She becomes

his favorite recreational companion, and he associates her with his most enjoyable moments of relaxation.

3. *Physical attractiveness.* She keeps herself physically fit and cares about her appearance in a way that her husband finds attractive.

4. *Domestic support.* She contributes to a home environment that offers a refuge from the stresses of life and encourages quality family time spent at home.

5. *Admiration and appreciation.* She respects and appreciates him more than anyone else. She reminds him of his value and achievements and helps him maintain self-confidence. She avoids criticizing him. She is proud of him not out of duty but based on a profound respect and appreciation for the man she has come to know better than anyone else.

When a man finds a woman who meets his five most important emotional needs, he will find her irresistible.

Discover Each Other's Most Important Emotional Needs

You may still be unsure that the emotional needs I've described are *your* most important needs—or the most important needs of your spouse. As I said, I cannot say for certain which of these needs apply to you or your spouse, so I've provided an opportunity for you and your spouse to find out for yourselves.

Appendix A contains a short description of each of the ten most important emotional needs. Then appendix B contains an Emotional Needs Questionnaire for both of you to complete. The questionnaire will help you determine which of the ten emotional needs are most important to you and your spouse.

Make two copies—one for you and one for your spouse—of the Emotional Needs Questionnaire. Make enlarged copies so you have space to write your answers. Before you complete them, be sure to read appendix A to become familiar with all ten emotional needs.

On the last page of the Emotional Needs Questionnaire, you have an opportunity to rank all ten needs in order of their importance to you. This final ranking helps your spouse put your emotional needs in perspective. They will know where to put the greatest effort to fulfill your happiness if you rank the needs honestly.

Avoid the temptation of putting only *unfulfilled* needs at the top of the list. Some of your most important needs may already be met. Don't use the list simply to get your spouse's attention; use it to accurately describe your needs. Remember, the needs at the top of the list should be those that give you the greatest pleasure when met and frustrate you the most when unmet.

I have been saying all along in this book that while both men and women share most of the ten basic needs, the order of their priorities is usually different. The top five needs of men are usually the bottom five of women, and the top five of women are usually the bottom five of men. When you indicate clearly the priority of your needs to your spouse, they can invest energy and attention where they do you the most good.

Few experiences compare with falling in love, but many couples fail to realize that love needs constant nurture and care. I've tried to give you some guidelines for providing that care and for building a marriage that sustains the feeling of love. If you've lost that feeling and must learn new skills to meet each other's emotional needs more effectively, it may be hard work at first. But after you've learned to be an expert husband and wife, your care for each other will become almost effortless. Take it from a man who's been in love for the entire fifty-eight years of his marriage—it's a lot less work to have a sensational marriage than it is to have a horrible marriage. When you and your spouse have learned how to meet each other's most important emotional needs, you will have mastered one of life's most valuable lessons.

Both you and your spouse should complete the questionnaire to help you both communicate your needs and how you've done at meeting them. With the increased understanding that comes through this communication, I hope you will build a long, passionate, and successful marriage.

The Ten Most Important Emotional Needs

Before you complete the Emotional Needs Questionnaire, review the following ten most important emotional needs.

Affection

Quite simply, affection is the expression of caring love. It symbolizes security and protection—vitally important ingredients in any relationship. When one spouse is affectionate to the other, the following messages are sent:

- I care about you. You are important to me, and I don't want anything to happen to you.
- I'm concerned about the problems you face, and I'll try to help you overcome them.

A hug can say these things. When we hug our friends and relatives, we are demonstrating our care for them. And there are other ways to show our affection—a greeting card, an "I love you" note, a bouquet of flowers, holding hands, walks after dinner, back rubs, phone calls, and conversations with thoughtful and loving expressions can all communicate affection.

Sex and affection are often confused, especially by men. Affection is an expression of care that is nonsexual and can be appropriately given to friends, relatives, children, and even pets. However, affectionate expressions, such as hugging and kissing, that are done with a sexual motive are actually sex, not affection.

Affection is, for many, the essential cement of a relationship. Without it, people can feel totally alienated. With it, they become emotionally bonded. If you feel terrific when your spouse is affectionate and you feel terrible when there is not enough affection, you have the emotional need for affection.

Sexual Fulfillment

Most people know whether they have a need for sex, but if you have any uncertainty, I will point out some of the most obvious symptoms.

Usually a sexual need predates your current relationship and is somewhat independent of your relationship. While you may have discovered a deep desire to make love to your spouse since you've been in love, it isn't quite the same thing as a sexual need. Wanting to make love when you are in love is sometimes merely a reflection of wanting to be emotionally and physically close.

Sexual fantasies are a dead giveaway for a sexual need. In general, fantasies are good indicators of emotional needs, with your most common fantasies reflecting your most important needs. If you have imagined what it would be like having your sexual need met in the most fulfilling ways, you probably have a sexual need. The more the fantasy is employed, the greater your need. And the way your sexual need is met in your fantasy can be a good indicator of your sexual predispositions and orientation.

When you married, you and your spouse both promised to be faithful to each other for life. This means that you agreed to be each other's only sexual partner "until death do us part." You made this commitment because you trusted each other to meet your sexual needs, to be sexually available and responsive. The need for sex, then, is a very exclusive need, and if you have it, you will be very dependent on your spouse to meet it for you. You have no other ethical choice.

Intimate Conversation

Intimate conversation is different from ordinary conversation. Its content focuses attention on very personal interests, problems, topics, and events. It's intimate because it reflects the caring love that you have for each other. You would generally not reveal such personal information to just anyone. Only those who seem to care about you and are willing to help you think through the problems you face are worthy of intimate conversation. If you have this need, whoever meets it best may deposit so many love units that you fall in love with that person. So if it's your need, be sure that your spouse is the one who meets it the best and most often.

Couples don't have too much difficulty talking to each other during courtship. That's a time of information gathering for both partners. Both are highly motivated to discover each other's likes and dislikes, personal background, current interests, and plans for the future. They are also willing to demonstrate their care for each other by trying to help solve problems that are raised.

But after marriage, many couples find that the spouse who would spend hours talking to them on the phone now seems to have lost all interest in talking to them and spends their spare time watching television or reading. Since the spouse's need for intimate conversation was fulfilled during courtship, they expect it to be met after marriage as well.

If you see conversation as a practical necessity, primarily as a means to an end, you probably don't have much of a need for it. But if you have a craving just to talk to someone about what's going on in your life, if you pick up your phone just because you feel like talking, if you enjoy conversation in its own right, consider intimate conversation to be one of your most important emotional needs.

Recreational Companionship

A need for recreational companionship combines two needs into one: the need to engage in recreational activities and the need to have a companion.

During your courtship, you and your spouse were probably each other's favorite recreational companions. It's not uncommon for one partner to join the other in activities they would never choose on their own. They simply want to spend as much time as possible with the person they like, and that means going where they go.

I won't deny that marriage changes a relationship considerably. But does it have to end the activities that helped make the relationship so compatible? Can't a husband's favorite recreational companion be his wife and vice versa?

If recreational activities are important to you and they are most fulfilling if someone joins you in them, include recreational companionship on your list of needs. Think about it for a moment in terms of the Love Bank. How much do you enjoy these activities, and how many love units would your spouse deposit whenever you enjoyed them together? What a waste it would be if all those love units were deposited into someone else's Love Bank account! And if it was the account of someone of the opposite sex, it would be downright dangerous.

Who should get credit for all the love units that are created when you are enjoying yourself recreationally? It's the one you should love the most, your spouse. That's precisely why I encourage a husband and a wife to be each other's favorite recreational companion. It's one of the simplest ways to deposit love units.

Honesty and Openness

Most of us want an honest relationship with our spouse. But some of us have a need for such a relationship because honesty and openness give us a sense of security.

To feel secure, we want accurate information about our spouse's thoughts, feelings, habits, likes, dislikes, personal history, daily activities, and plans for the future. If a spouse does not provide honest and open communication, trust can be undermined and the feelings of security can eventually be destroyed. Then their partner can't trust the signals that are being sent and has no foundation on which to build a solid relationship. Instead of adjusting to each other, spouses feel off balance; instead of growing together, they grow apart.

Aside from the practical considerations of honesty and openness, there are some of us who feel happy and fulfilled when our spouse reveals their most private thoughts to us. And we feel very frustrated when they are hidden. That reaction is evidence of an emotional need, one that can and should be met in marriage.

Physical Attractiveness

For many people, physical appearance can become one of the greatest sources of love units. If you have this need, an attractive person not only will get your attention but also may distract you from whatever you're doing. In fact, that's what may have first drawn you to your spouse—their physical appearance.

Some people consider this need to be temporary and important only in the beginning of a relationship. After two people get to know each other better, some feel that physical attractiveness usually takes a backseat to deeper and more intimate needs. But that has not been my experience, nor has it been the experience of many people I've counseled, particularly men. For many, the need for physical attractiveness continues throughout marriage, and just seeing the spouse looking attractive deposits love units.

Among the various aspects of physical attractiveness, weight generally gets the most attention. However, choice of clothing, hairstyle, makeup, and personal hygiene also come together to make a person attractive. It can be very subjective, and you are the judge of what is attractive to you.

If the attractiveness of your spouse makes you feel great and a loss of that attractiveness would make you feel very frustrated, you should probably include this category on your list of most important emotional needs.

Financial Support

Many people marry partially for the financial security their spouse provides them. In other words, part of the reason they marry is for financial support. Is financial support one of your most important emotional needs?

If may be difficult for you to know if you have a need for financial support, especially if your spouse has always been gainfully employed. But what if, before marriage, your spouse had told you not to expect any income from them? Would it have affected your decision to marry? Or what if your spouse could not find work, and you had to support them financially throughout life? Would that withdraw love units?

You may have a need for financial support if you expect your spouse to earn a living. But you definitely have that need if you do not expect to be earning a living yourself, at least during part of your marriage.

What constitutes financial support? Earning enough to buy everything you could possibly desire or earning just enough to get by? Different spouses would answer this differently, and the same spouse might answer differently in different stages of life. But like many of these emotional needs, financial support is sometimes difficult to discuss. As a result, many spouses have hidden expectations, assumptions, and resentments. Try to understand what you expect from your spouse financially to feel fulfilled. And what would it take for you to feel frustrated? Your analysis will help you determine if you have a need for financial support.

Domestic Support

The need for domestic support is a time bomb. At first, it seems irrelevant, a throwback to more primitive times. But for many couples, the need explodes after a few years of marriage, surprising both husband and wife.

In earlier generations, it was assumed that all husbands had this need and that all wives would naturally meet it. Times have changed, and needs have changed along with them. Now, many of the men I counsel would rather have their wives meet their needs for affection or conversation, needs that have traditionally been more characteristic of women. And many women, especially career women, gain a great deal of pleasure having their husbands create a peaceful and well-managed home environment.

Marriage usually begins with a willingness of both spouses to share domestic responsibilities. It's common for newlyweds to divide many household tasks. The groom welcomes his wife's help in doing what he had to do by himself as a bachelor. At this point in marriage, neither of them would identify domestic support as an important emotional need. But the time bomb is ticking.

When does the need for domestic support explode? When the children arrive! Children create huge needs—both a greater need for income and more domestic responsibilities. The previous division of labor becomes obsolete. Both spouses must take on new responsibilities—and which ones will they take?

Domestic support includes cooking meals, getting groceries, washing clothes, cleaning the house, and childcare. If you feel very fulfilled when your spouse does these things or takes charge of getting them done and very annoyed when they are not done, you have the need for domestic support.

Family Commitment

In addition to creating a greater need for income and more domestic responsibilities, the arrival of children creates in many people the need for family commitment. Again, if you don't have children yet, you may not sense this need, but when the first child arrives, a change may take place that you didn't anticipate.

Family commitment is not childcare—feeding, clothing, or watching over children to keep them safe. Childcare falls under the category of domestic support. Family commitment, on the other hand, is a responsibility for the development of the children, teaching them the values of thoughtfulness and care for each other. It is spending quality time with your children to help them develop into successful adults.

Evidence of this need is a craving for your spouse's involvement in the moral and educational development of your children. When they help care for the children, you feel very fulfilled, and when they neglect the children's development, you feel very frustrated.

We all want our children to be successful, but if you have the need for family commitment, your spouse's participation in family activities will make large Love Bank deposits. And your spouse's neglect of your children will make noticeable withdrawals.

Admiration and Appreciation

If you have the need for admiration and appreciation, you may have fallen in love with your spouse partly because of their compliments to you. Some people just love to be told that they are appreciated. Your spouse may also have been careful not to criticize you. If you have a need for admiration, the slightest criticism may hurt you deeply.

Many of us have a deep desire to be respected, valued, and appreciated by our spouse. We need to be affirmed clearly and often. There's nothing wrong with feeling this way. Even God wants us to appreciate him!

Appreciation is one of the easiest needs to meet. Just a compliment, and presto, you've made your spouse's day. On the other hand, it's also easy to be critical. A trivial word of rebuke can be very upsetting to some people, ruining their day and withdrawing love units at an alarming rate.

Your spouse may have the power to build up or deplete their account in your Love Bank with just a few words. If you can be affected that easily, be sure to add admiration and appreciation to your list of most important emotional needs.

Emotional Needs Questionnaire

This questionnaire is designed to help you determine your most important emotional needs and evaluate your spouse's effectiveness in meeting those needs. Answer all the questions as candidly as possible. Do not try to minimize any needs that you feel have been unmet. If your answers require more space, use and attach a separate sheet of paper.

Your spouse should complete the Emotional Needs Questionnaire so that you can discover their needs and evaluate your effectiveness in meeting those needs.

When you have completed this questionnaire, go through it a second time to be certain your answers accurately reflect your feelings. Do not erase your original answers, but cross them out lightly so that your spouse can see the corrections and discuss them with you.

The final page of this questionnaire asks you to identify and rank five of the ten needs in order of their importance to you. The most important emotional needs are those that give you the most pleasure when met and frustrate you the most when unmet. Resist the temptation to identify as most important only those needs that your spouse is not presently meeting. Include *all* your emotional needs in your consideration of those that are most important.

1. Affection: the nonsexual expression of extraordinary care through words, cards, gifts, hugs, kisses, and courtesies.

   A. Need for affection: indicate how much you need affection by circling the appropriate number.

0	1	2	3	4	5	6

   I have no need   I have a moderate need   I have a great need

   B. Evaluation of spouse's affection: indicate your satisfaction with your spouse's affection by circling the appropriate number.

-3	-2	-1	0	1	2	3

   I am extremely satisfied   I am neither satisfied   I am extremely dissatisfied
                     or dissatisfied

   My spouse gives me all the affection I need. ☐ Yes ☐ No

   If your answer is no, how often would you like your spouse to be affectionate with you? _____ times each day/week/month.
             (write number)   (circle one)

   I like the way my spouse provides affection. ☐ Yes ☐ No

   If your answer is no, which of the following would you like to see improved? Circle the letters that apply to you.

a. words (e.g., I love you)	e. courtesies
b. cards/gifts/flowers	f. help with problems
c. touch (e.g., back rubs)	g. tone of voice
d. hugs/kisses	h. other _____

   If you circled any of these, explain how your need for affection in each example could be better satisfied in your marriage. Use an extra sheet of paper if necessary.

   _____

   _____

   _____

2. Sexual fulfillment: sexual experiences that are predictably enjoyable and frequent.

   A. Need for sexual fulfillment: indicate how much you need sexual fulfillment by circling the appropriate number.

0	1	2	3	4	5	6
I have no need			I have a moderate need			I have a great need

   B. Evaluation of spouse's sexual fulfillment: indicate your satisfaction with your spouse's sexual fulfillment by circling the appropriate number.

-3	-2	-1	0	1	2	3
I am extremely satisfied			I am neither satisfied or dissatisfied			I am extremely dissatisfied

   My spouse has sex with me as often as I need.   ☐ Yes   ☐ No

   If your answer is no, how often would you like your spouse to have sex with you? _____ times each day/week/month.
      (write number)   (circle one)

   I like the way my spouse has sex with me.   ☐ Yes   ☐ No

   If your answer is no, which of the following would you like to see improved? Circle the letters that apply to you.

   a. understanding each other's sexual responses

   b. learning to bring out the best of those responses

   c. creating a mutually satisfying and enjoyable sexual experience

   d. other _____

   If you circled any of these, explain how your need for sexual fulfillment in each example could be better satisfied in your marriage. Use an extra sheet of paper if necessary.

   _____

   _____

   _____

3. Intimate conversation: sharing feelings, discussing topics of personal interest/opinions, and making plans in a way that expresses extraordinary care.

A. Need for intimate conversation: indicate how much you need intimate conversation by circling the appropriate number.

0	1	2	3	4	5	6

I have no need   I have a moderate need   I have a great need

B. Evaluation of spouse's intimate conversation: indicate your satisfaction with your spouse's intimate conversation by circling the appropriate number.

-3	-2	-1	0	1	2	3

I am extremely satisfied   I am neither satisfied or dissatisfied   I am extremely dissatisfied

My spouse engages in intimate conversation with me as often as I need.
☐ Yes   ☐ No

If your answer is no, how often would you like your spouse to engage in intimate conversation with you? _____ times each day/week/month.
(write number)   (circle one)

I like the way my spouse talks to me during intimate conversation.
☐ Yes   ☐ No

If your answer is no, which of the following would you like to see improved? Circle the letters that apply to you.

a. use conversation to under-stand each other

b. develop interest in each other's favorite topics

c. balance the conversation

d. give undivided attention

e. avoid demands

f. avoid disrespect

g. avoid anger

h. avoid dwelling on mistakes

i. other _____

If you circled any of these, explain how your need for intimate conversation in each example could be better satisfied in your marriage. Use an extra sheet of paper if necessary.

_____

_____

4. Recreational companionship: leisure activities with at least one other person.

A. Need for recreational companionship: indicate how much you need recreational companionship by circling the appropriate number.

0	1	2	3	4	5	6

I have no need   I have a moderate need   I have a great need

B. Evaluation of spouse's recreational companionship: indicate your satisfaction with your spouse's recreational companionship by circling the appropriate number.

-3	-2	-1	0	1	2	3

I am extremely satisfied   I am neither satisfied or dissatisfied   I am extremely dissatisfied

My spouse joins me in recreational activities as often as I need.
☐ Yes ☐ No

If your answer is no, how often would you like your spouse to join you in recreational activities? _____ times each day/week/month.
(write number)   (circle one)

I like the way my spouse engages in recreational activities with me.
☐ Yes ☐ No

If your answer is no, which of the following would you like to see improved? Circle the letters that apply to you.

a. identify mutually enjoyable recreational activities

b. develop skill in mutually enjoyable recreational activities

c. other _____

If you circled any of these, explain how your need for recreational companionship in each example could be better satisfied in your marriage. Use an extra sheet of paper if necessary.

_____

_____

_____

5. Honesty and openness: truthful and frank expression of positive and negative feelings, events of the past, daily events and schedule, and plans for the future; not leaving a false impression.

A. Need for honesty and openness: indicate how much you need honesty and openness by circling the appropriate number.

0	1	2	3	4	5	6

I have no need   I have a moderate need   I have a great need

B. Evaluation of spouse's honesty and openness: indicate your satisfaction with your spouse's honesty and openness by circling the appropriate number.

-3	-2	-1	0	1	2	3

I am extremely satisfied I am neither satisfied I am extremely dissatisfied
         or dissatisfied

I like the way my spouse is honest and open with me. ☐ Yes ☐ No

If your answer is no, which of the following would you like to see improved? Circle the letters that apply to you.

 a. sharing positive and negative emotional reactions to significant aspects of life

 b. sharing information regarding their personal history

 c. sharing information about their daily activities

 d. sharing information about their future plans

 e. other _____

If you circled any of these, explain how your need for honesty and openness in each example could be better satisfied in your marriage. Use an extra sheet of paper if necessary.

_____

_____

_____

6. Physical attractiveness: physical traits of the opposite sex that are aesthetically and/or sexually pleasing to you.

A. Need for physical attractiveness: indicate how much you need physical attractiveness in your spouse by circling the appropriate number.

0	1	2	3	4	5	6
I have no need			I have a moderate need			I have a great need

B. Evaluation of spouse's physical attractiveness: indicate your satisfaction with your spouse's physical attractiveness by circling the appropriate number.

-3	-2	-1	0	1	2	3
I am extremely satisfied			I am neither satisfied or dissatisfied			I am extremely dissatisfied

I like the way my spouse looks. ☐ Yes ☐ No

If your answer is no, which of the following would you like to see improved? Circle the letters that apply to you.

a. physical fitness

b. weight

c. clothing style

d. hairstyle

e. physical hygiene

f. other _____

If you circled any of these, explain how your need for physical attractiveness in each example could be better satisfied in your marriage. Use an extra sheet of paper if necessary.

_____

_____

_____

7. Financial support: provision of the financial resources to help house, feed, and clothe your family at a standard of living acceptable to you.

A. Need for financial support: indicate how much you need financial support by circling the appropriate number.

0	1	2	3	4	5	6

I have no need   I have a moderate need   I have a great need

B. Evaluation of spouse's financial support: indicate your satisfaction with your spouse's financial support by circling the appropriate number.

-3	-2	-1	0	1	2	3

I am extremely satisfied   I am neither satisfied or dissatisfied   I am extremely dissatisfied

I like the way my spouse provides financial support.   ☐ Yes   ☐ No

If your answer is no, which of the following would you like to see improved? Circle the letters that apply to you.

     a. salary

     b. work travel

     c. family budget

     d. work hours

     e. choice of career

     f. other _____

If you circled any of these, explain how your need for financial support in each example could be better satisfied in your marriage. Use an extra sheet of paper if necessary.

_____

_____

_____

8. Domestic support: provision of help with household tasks and childcare.

A. Need for domestic support: indicate how much you need domestic support by circling the appropriate number.

0	1	2	3	4	5	6

I have no need   I have a moderate need   I have a great need

B. Evaluation of spouse's domestic support: indicate your satisfaction with your spouse's domestic support by circling the appropriate number.

-3	-2	-1	0	1	2	3

I am extremely satisfied   I am neither satisfied   I am extremely dissatisfied
                              or dissatisfied

My spouse provides domestic support as often as I need   ☐ Yes   ☐ No

If your answer is no, how often would you like your spouse to provide domestic support? _____ times each day/week/month.
                         (write number)   (circle one)

I like the way my spouse provides domestic support.   ☐ Yes   ☐ No

If your answer is no, which of the following would you like to see improved? Circle the letters that apply to you.

a. housecleaning

b. tidiness

c. yard/exterior work

d. laundry

e. household shopping

f. childcare

g. cooking/kitchen cleanup

h. other _____

If you circled any of these, explain how your need for domestic support in each example could be better satisfied in your marriage. Use an extra sheet of paper if necessary.

_____

_____

_____

9. Family commitment: involvement in the moral and educational development of the children.

A. Need for family commitment: indicate how much you need family commitment by circling the appropriate number.

```
0          1          2          3          4          5          6
|··········|··········|··········|··········|··········|··········|
I have no need          I have a moderate need          I have a great need
```

B. Evaluation of spouse's family commitment: indicate your satisfaction with your spouse's family commitment by circling the appropriate number.

```
-3        -2        -1         0         1         2         3
|··········|··········|··········|··········|··········|··········|
I am extremely satisfied    I am neither satisfied    I am extremely dissatisfied
                            or dissatisfied
```

My spouse shows family commitment as often as I need. ☐ Yes ☐ No

If your answer is no, how often would you like your spouse to show family commitment? _____ times each day/week/month.
       (write number)   (circle one)

I like the way my spouse shows family commitment. ☐ Yes ☐ No

If your answer is no, which of the following would you like to see improved? Circle the letters that apply to you.

a. time spent with family

b. partnership in children's moral development

c. partnership in discipline methods

d. family outings (walks, bike rides, etc.)

e. family projects

f. family mealtime

g. help with school-related needs

h. other _____

If you circled any of these, explain how your need for family commitment in each example could be better satisfied in your marriage. Use an extra sheet of paper if necessary.

_____

_____

10. Admiration and appreciation: being shown respect and value.

A. Need for admiration and appreciation: indicate how much you need admiration and appreciation by circling the appropriate number.

0	1	2	3	4	5	6

I have no need   I have a moderate need   I have a great need

B. Evaluation of spouse's admiration and appreciation: indicate your satisfaction with your spouse's admiration and appreciation by circling the appropriate number.

-3	-2	-1	0	1	2	3

I am extremely satisfied   I am neither satisfied   I am extremely dissatisfied
                       or dissatisfied

My spouse shows admiration and appreciation as often as I need.

☐ Yes   ☐ No

If your answer is no, how often would you like your spouse to show admiration and appreciation? _____ times each day/week/month.
                                (write number)   (circle one)

I like the way my spouse shows admiration and appreciation.

☐ Yes   ☐ No

If your answer is no, which of the following would you like to see improved? Circle the letters that apply to you.

Expressions of Admiration

a. with me, privately   c. being critical and/or judgmental of me, privately

b. with me, publicly   d. being critical and/or judgmental of me, publicly

Expressions of Appreciation

a. with me, privately   b. with me, publicly

If you circled any of these, explain how your need for admiration and appreciation in each example could be better satisfied in your marriage. Use an extra sheet of paper if necessary.

_____

_____

Ranking Your Emotional Needs

The ten basic emotional needs are listed below. There is also space for you to add other emotional needs that you feel are essential to your marital happiness.

In the space provided in front of each need, write a 1 before the most important need, a 2 before the next most important need, and so on until you have ranked your five most important needs.

To help you rank these needs, imagine that you will have only one need met in your marriage. Which would make you the happiest, knowing that all the others would go unmet? That need should be 1. If only two needs will be met, what would your second selection be? Which five needs, when met, would make you the happiest?

_____ affection

_____ sexual fulfillment

_____ intimate conversation

_____ recreational companionship

_____ honesty and openness

_____ physical attractiveness

_____ financial support

_____ domestic support

_____ family commitment

_____ admiration and appreciation

_____ _____

_____ _____

_____ _____

_____ _____

Appendix C

Recreational Enjoyment Inventory

Please indicate how much you enjoy, or think you might enjoy, each recreational activity listed below. In the space provided by each activity, under the appropriate column (husband's or wife's), circle one of the numbers to reflect your feelings: 3 = very enjoyable; 2 = enjoyable; 1 = somewhat enjoyable; 0 = no feelings one way or the other; -1 = somewhat unpleasant; -2 = unpleasant; -3 = very unpleasant. Add to the list, in the spaces provided, activities you would enjoy that are not listed. In the fourth column, add the ratings of both you and your spouse *only if both ratings are positive*. The activities with the highest sum are those that you should select when planning recreational time together.

Activity	Husband's Rating	Wife's Rating	Total Rating
Acting	-3 • -2 • -1 • 0 • 1 • 2 • 3	-3 • -2 • -1 • 0 • 1 • 2 • 3	_____
Aerobic exercise	-3 • -2 • -1 • 0 • 1 • 2 • 3	-3 • -2 • -1 • 0 • 1 • 2 • 3	_____
Amusement parks	-3 • -2 • -1 • 0 • 1 • 2 • 3	-3 • -2 • -1 • 0 • 1 • 2 • 3	_____
Antique collecting	-3 • -2 • -1 • 0 • 1 • 2 • 3	-3 • -2 • -1 • 0 • 1 • 2 • 3	_____
Archery	-3 • -2 • -1 • 0 • 1 • 2 • 3	-3 • -2 • -1 • 0 • 1 • 2 • 3	_____
Astronomy	-3 • -2 • -1 • 0 • 1 • 2 • 3	-3 • -2 • -1 • 0 • 1 • 2 • 3	_____
Auto customizing	-3 • -2 • -1 • 0 • 1 • 2 • 3	-3 • -2 • -1 • 0 • 1 • 2 • 3	_____
Auto racing (watching)	-3 • -2 • -1 • 0 • 1 • 2 • 3	-3 • -2 • -1 • 0 • 1 • 2 • 3	_____

Activity	Husband's Rating	Wife's Rating	Total Rating
Badminton	-3 • -2 • -1 • 0 • 1 • 2 • 3	-3 • -2 • -1 • 0 • 1 • 2 • 3	_____
Baseball (playing)	-3 • -2 • -1 • 0 • 1 • 2 • 3	-3 • -2 • -1 • 0 • 1 • 2 • 3	_____
Baseball (watching)	-3 • -2 • -1 • 0 • 1 • 2 • 3	-3 • -2 • -1 • 0 • 1 • 2 • 3	_____
Basketball (playing)	-3 • -2 • -1 • 0 • 1 • 2 • 3	-3 • -2 • -1 • 0 • 1 • 2 • 3	_____
Basketball (watching)	-3 • -2 • -1 • 0 • 1 • 2 • 3	-3 • -2 • -1 • 0 • 1 • 2 • 3	_____
Bible study	-3 • -2 • -1 • 0 • 1 • 2 • 3	-3 • -2 • -1 • 0 • 1 • 2 • 3	_____
Bicycling	-3 • -2 • -1 • 0 • 1 • 2 • 3	-3 • -2 • -1 • 0 • 1 • 2 • 3	_____
Board games	-3 • -2 • -1 • 0 • 1 • 2 • 3	-3 • -2 • -1 • 0 • 1 • 2 • 3	_____
Boating	-3 • -2 • -1 • 0 • 1 • 2 • 3	-3 • -2 • -1 • 0 • 1 • 2 • 3	_____
Bodybuilding	-3 • -2 • -1 • 0 • 1 • 2 • 3	-3 • -2 • -1 • 0 • 1 • 2 • 3	_____
Bowling	-3 • -2 • -1 • 0 • 1 • 2 • 3	-3 • -2 • -1 • 0 • 1 • 2 • 3	_____
Boxing (watching)	-3 • -2 • -1 • 0 • 1 • 2 • 3	-3 • -2 • -1 • 0 • 1 • 2 • 3	_____
Camping	-3 • -2 • -1 • 0 • 1 • 2 • 3	-3 • -2 • -1 • 0 • 1 • 2 • 3	_____
Canoeing	-3 • -2 • -1 • 0 • 1 • 2 • 3	-3 • -2 • -1 • 0 • 1 • 2 • 3	_____
Card games	3 • -2 • -1 • 0 • 1 • 2 • 3	-3 • -2 • -1 • 0 • 1 • 2 • 3	_____
Checkers	-3 • -2 • -1 • 0 • 1 • 2 • 3	-3 • -2 • -1 • 0 • 1 • 2 • 3	_____
Chess	-3 • -2 • -1 • 0 • 1 • 2 • 3	-3 • -2 • -1 • 0 • 1 • 2 • 3	_____
Church services	-3 • -2 • -1 • 0 • 1 • 2 • 3	-3 • -2 • -1 • 0 • 1 • 2 • 3	_____
Coin collecting	-3 • -2 • -1 • 0 • 1 • 2 • 3	-3 • -2 • -1 • 0 • 1 • 2 • 3	_____
Computer games	-3 • -2 • -1 • 0 • 1 • 2 • 3	-3 • -2 • -1 • 0 • 1 • 2 • 3	_____
Computer programming	-3 • -2 • -1 • 0 • 1 • 2 • 3	-3 • -2 • -1 • 0 • 1 • 2 • 3	_____
Computer _____	-3 • -2 • -1 • 0 • 1 • 2 • 3	-3 • -2 • -1 • 0 • 1 • 2 • 3	_____
Concerts (classical music)	-3 • -2 • -1 • 0 • 1 • 2 • 3	-3 • -2 • -1 • 0 • 1 • 2 • 3	_____
Concerts (country music)	-3 • -2 • -1 • 0 • 1 • 2 • 3	-3 • -2 • -1 • 0 • 1 • 2 • 3	_____
Concerts (rock music)	-3 • -2 • -1 • 0 • 1 • 2 • 3	-3 • -2 • -1 • 0 • 1 • 2 • 3	_____
Croquet	-3 • -2 • -1 • 0 • 1 • 2 • 3	-3 • -2 • -1 • 0 • 1 • 2 • 3	_____
Dancing (ballroom)	-3 • -2 • -1 • 0 • 1 • 2 • 3	-3 • -2 • -1 • 0 • 1 • 2 • 3	_____
Dancing (rock)	-3 • -2 • -1 • 0 • 1 • 2 • 3	-3 • -2 • -1 • 0 • 1 • 2 • 3	_____
Dancing (square)	-3 • -2 • -1 • 0 • 1 • 2 • 3	-3 • -2 • -1 • 0 • 1 • 2 • 3	_____
Dancing (_____)	-3 • -2 • -1 • 0 • 1 • 2 • 3	-3 • -2 • -1 • 0 • 1 • 2 • 3	_____
Dining out	-3 • -2 • -1 • 0 • 1 • 2 • 3	-3 • -2 • -1 • 0 • 1 • 2 • 3	_____
Fishing	-3 • -2 • -1 • 0 • 1 • 2 • 3	-3 • -2 • -1 • 0 • 1 • 2 • 3	_____
Football (playing)	-3 • -2 • -1 • 0 • 1 • 2 • 3	-3 • -2 • -1 • 0 • 1 • 2 • 3	_____

Recreational Enjoyment Inventory

Activity	Husband's Rating	Wife's Rating	Total Rating
Football (watching)	-3 • -2 • -1 • 0 • 1 • 2 • 3	-3 • -2 • -1 • 0 • 1 • 2 • 3	_____
Gardening	-3 • -2 • -1 • 0 • 1 • 2 • 3	-3 • -2 • -1 • 0 • 1 • 2 • 3	_____
Genealogical research	-3 • -2 • -1 • 0 • 1 • 2 • 3	-3 • -2 • -1 • 0 • 1 • 2 • 3	_____
Golf	-3 • -2 • -1 • 0 • 1 • 2 • 3	-3 • -2 • -1 • 0 • 1 • 2 • 3	_____
Handball	-3 • -2 • -1 • 0 • 1 • 2 • 3	-3 • -2 • -1 • 0 • 1 • 2 • 3	_____
Hiking	-3 • -2 • -1 • 0 • 1 • 2 • 3	-3 • -2 • -1 • 0 • 1 • 2 • 3	_____
Hockey (playing)	-3 • -2 • -1 • 0 • 1 • 2 • 3	-3 • -2 • -1 • 0 • 1 • 2 • 3	_____
Hockey (watching)	-3 • -2 • -1 • 0 • 1 • 2 • 3	-3 • -2 • -1 • 0 • 1 • 2 • 3	_____
Horseback riding	-3 • -2 • -1 • 0 • 1 • 2 • 3	-3 • -2 • -1 • 0 • 1 • 2 • 3	_____
Horse racing (watching)	-3 • -2 • -1 • 0 • 1 • 2 • 3	-3 • -2 • -1 • 0 • 1 • 2 • 3	_____
Horseshoe pitching	-3 • -2 • -1 • 0 • 1 • 2 • 3	-3 • -2 • -1 • 0 • 1 • 2 • 3	_____
Horse shows (watching)	-3 • -2 • -1 • 0 • 1 • 2 • 3	-3 • -2 • -1 • 0 • 1 • 2 • 3	_____
Hot-air ballooning	-3 • -2 • -1 • 0 • 1 • 2 • 3	-3 • -2 • -1 • 0 • 1 • 2 • 3	_____
Hunting	-3 • -2 • -1 • 0 • 1 • 2 • 3	-3 • -2 • -1 • 0 • 1 • 2 • 3	_____
Ice fishing	-3 • -2 • -1 • 0 • 1 • 2 • 3	-3 • -2 • -1 • 0 • 1 • 2 • 3	_____
Ice-skating	-3 • -2 • -1 • 0 • 1 • 2 • 3	-3 • -2 • -1 • 0 • 1 • 2 • 3	_____
Jogging	-3 • -2 • -1 • 0 • 1 • 2 • 3	-3 • -2 • -1 • 0 • 1 • 2 • 3	_____
Judo	-3 • -2 • -1 • 0 • 1 • 2 • 3	-3 • -2 • -1 • 0 • 1 • 2 • 3	_____
Karate	-3 • -2 • -1 • 0 • 1 • 2 • 3	-3 • -2 • -1 • 0 • 1 • 2 • 3	_____
Knitting	-3 • -2 • -1 • 0 • 1 • 2 • 3	-3 • -2 • -1 • 0 • 1 • 2 • 3	_____
Metalwork	-3 • -2 • -1 • 0 • 1 • 2 • 3	-3 • -2 • -1 • 0 • 1 • 2 • 3	_____
Model building	-3 • -2 • -1 • 0 • 1 • 2 • 3	-3 • -2 • -1 • 0 • 1 • 2 • 3	_____
Mountain climbing	-3 • -2 • -1 • 0 • 1 • 2 • 3	-3 • -2 • -1 • 0 • 1 • 2 • 3	_____
Movies	-3 • -2 • -1 • 0 • 1 • 2 • 3	-3 • -2 • -1 • 0 • 1 • 2 • 3	_____
Museums	-3 • -2 • -1 • 0 • 1 • 2 • 3	-3 • -2 • -1 • 0 • 1 • 2 • 3	_____
Opera	-3 • -2 • -1 • 0 • 1 • 2 • 3	-3 • -2 • -1 • 0 • 1 • 2 • 3	_____
Painting	-3 • -2 • -1 • 0 • 1 • 2 • 3	-3 • -2 • -1 • 0 • 1 • 2 • 3	_____
Photography	-3 • -2 • -1 • 0 • 1 • 2 • 3	-3 • -2 • -1 • 0 • 1 • 2 • 3	_____
Plays	-3 • -2 • -1 • 0 • 1 • 2 • 3	-3 • -2 • -1 • 0 • 1 • 2 • 3	_____
Pool (billiards)	-3 • -2 • -1 • 0 • 1 • 2 • 3	-3 • -2 • -1 • 0 • 1 • 2 • 3	_____
Quilting	-3 • -2 • -1 • 0 • 1 • 2 • 3	-3 • -2 • -1 • 0 • 1 • 2 • 3	_____
Racquetball	-3 • -2 • -1 • 0 • 1 • 2 • 3	-3 • -2 • -1 • 0 • 1 • 2 • 3	_____
Remodeling (home)	-3 • -2 • -1 • 0 • 1 • 2 • 3	-3 • -2 • -1 • 0 • 1 • 2 • 3	_____

Activity	Husband's Rating	Wife's Rating	Total Rating
Rock collecting	-3 • -2 • -1 • 0 • 1 • 2 • 3	-3 • -2 • -1 • 0 • 1 • 2 • 3	_____
Roller-blading	-3 • -2 • -1 • 0 • 1 • 2 • 3	-3 • -2 • -1 • 0 • 1 • 2 • 3	_____
Rowing	-3 • -2 • -1 • 0 • 1 • 2 • 3	-3 • -2 • -1 • 0 • 1 • 2 • 3	_____
Sailing	-3 • -2 • -1 • 0 • 1 • 2 • 3	-3 • -2 • -1 • 0 • 1 • 2 • 3	_____
Scuba diving (snorkeling)	-3 • -2 • -1 • 0 • 1 • 2 • 3	-3 • -2 • -1 • 0 • 1 • 2 • 3	_____
Sculpting	-3 • -2 • -1 • 0 • 1 • 2 • 3	-3 • -2 • -1 • 0 • 1 • 2 • 3	_____
Shooting (pistol)	-3 • -2 • -1 • 0 • 1 • 2 • 3	-3 • -2 • -1 • 0 • 1 • 2 • 3	_____
Shooting (skeet, trap)	-3 • -2 • -1 • 0 • 1 • 2 • 3	-3 • -2 • -1 • 0 • 1 • 2 • 3	_____
Shopping (clothes)	-3 • -2 • -1 • 0 • 1 • 2 • 3	-3 • -2 • -1 • 0 • 1 • 2 • 3	_____
Shopping (groceries)	-3 • -2 • -1 • 0 • 1 • 2 • 3	-3 • -2 • -1 • 0 • 1 • 2 • 3	_____
Shopping (vehicles)	-3 • -2 • -1 • 0 • 1 • 2 • 3	-3 • -2 • -1 • 0 • 1 • 2 • 3	_____
Shopping (_____)	-3 • -2 • -1 • 0 • 1 • 2 • 3	-3 • -2 • -1 • 0 • 1 • 2 • 3	_____
Shuffleboard	-3 • -2 • -1 • 0 • 1 • 2 • 3	-3 • -2 • -1 • 0 • 1 • 2 • 3	_____
Sightseeing	-3 • -2 • -1 • 0 • 1 • 2 • 3	-3 • -2 • -1 • 0 • 1 • 2 • 3	_____
Singing	-3 • -2 • -1 • 0 • 1 • 2 • 3	-3 • -2 • -1 • 0 • 1 • 2 • 3	_____
Skiing (cross-country)	-3 • -2 • -1 • 0 • 1 • 2 • 3	-3 • -2 • -1 • 0 • 1 • 2 • 3	_____
Skiing (downhill)	-3 • -2 • -1 • 0 • 1 • 2 • 3	-3 • -2 • -1 • 0 • 1 • 2 • 3	_____
Skiing (water)	-3 • -2 • -1 • 0 • 1 • 2 • 3	-3 • -2 • -1 • 0 • 1 • 2 • 3	_____
Skydiving	-3 • -2 • -1 • 0 • 1 • 2 • 3	-3 • -2 • -1 • 0 • 1 • 2 • 3	_____
Snowmobiling	-3 • -2 • -1 • 0 • 1 • 2 • 3	-3 • -2 • -1 • 0 • 1 • 2 • 3	_____
Softball (playing)	-3 • -2 • -1 • 0 • 1 • 2 • 3	-3 • -2 • -1 • 0 • 1 • 2 • 3	_____
Softball (watching)	-3 • -2 • -1 • 0 • 1 • 2 • 3	-3 • -2 • -1 • 0 • 1 • 2 • 3	_____
Stamp collecting	-3 • -2 • -1 • 0 • 1 • 2 • 3	-3 • -2 • -1 • 0 • 1 • 2 • 3	_____
Surfing	-3 • -2 • -1 • 0 • 1 • 2 • 3	-3 • -2 • -1 • 0 • 1 • 2 • 3	_____
Swimming	-3 • -2 • -1 • 0 • 1 • 2 • 3	-3 • -2 • -1 • 0 • 1 • 2 • 3	_____
Table tennis	-3 • -2 • -1 • 0 • 1 • 2 • 3	-3 • -2 • -1 • 0 • 1 • 2 • 3	_____
Taxidermy	-3 • -2 • -1 • 0 • 1 • 2 • 3	-3 • -2 • -1 • 0 • 1 • 2 • 3	_____
Television	-3 • -2 • -1 • 0 • 1 • 2 • 3	-3 • -2 • -1 • 0 • 1 • 2 • 3	_____
Tennis	-3 • -2 • -1 • 0 • 1 • 2 • 3	-3 • -2 • -1 • 0 • 1 • 2 • 3	_____
Tobogganing	-3 • -2 • -1 • 0 • 1 • 2 • 3	-3 • -2 • -1 • 0 • 1 • 2 • 3	_____
Video games	-3 • -2 • -1 • 0 • 1 • 2 • 3	-3 • -2 • -1 • 0 • 1 • 2 • 3	_____
Video production (on social media)	-3 • -2 • -1 • 0 • 1 • 2 • 3	-3 • -2 • -1 • 0 • 1 • 2 • 3	_____

Recreational Enjoyment Inventory

Activity	Husband's Rating	Wife's Rating	Total Rating
Volleyball	-3 • -2 • -1 • 0 • 1 • 2 • 3	-3 • -2 • -1 • 0 • 1 • 2 • 3	_____
Weaving	-3 • -2 • -1 • 0 • 1 • 2 • 3	-3 • -2 • -1 • 0 • 1 • 2 • 3	_____
Woodworking	-3 • -2 • -1 • 0 • 1 • 2 • 3	-3 • -2 • -1 • 0 • 1 • 2 • 3	_____
Wrestling (watching)	-3 • -2 • -1 • 0 • 1 • 2 • 3	-3 • -2 • -1 • 0 • 1 • 2 • 3	_____
Yachting	-3 • -2 • -1 • 0 • 1 • 2 • 3	-3 • -2 • -1 • 0 • 1 • 2 • 3	_____
_____	-3 • -2 • -1 • 0 • 1 • 2 • 3	-3 • -2 • -1 • 0 • 1 • 2 • 3	_____
_____	-3 • -2 • -1 • 0 • 1 • 2 • 3	-3 • -2 • -1 • 0 • 1 • 2 • 3	_____
_____	-3 • -2 • -1 • 0 • 1 • 2 • 3	-3 • -2 • -1 • 0 • 1 • 2 • 3	_____
_____	-3 • -2 • -1 • 0 • 1 • 2 • 3	-3 • -2 • -1 • 0 • 1 • 2 • 3	_____
_____	-3 • -2 • -1 • 0 • 1 • 2 • 3	-3 • -2 • -1 • 0 • 1 • 2 • 3	_____
_____	-3 • -2 • -1 • 0 • 1 • 2 • 3	-3 • -2 • -1 • 0 • 1 • 2 • 3	_____
_____	-3 • -2 • -1 • 0 • 1 • 2 • 3	-3 • -2 • -1 • 0 • 1 • 2 • 3	_____
_____	-3 • -2 • -1 • 0 • 1 • 2 • 3	-3 • -2 • -1 • 0 • 1 • 2 • 3	_____
_____	-3 • -2 • -1 • 0 • 1 • 2 • 3	-3 • -2 • -1 • 0 • 1 • 2 • 3	_____
_____	-3 • -2 • -1 • 0 • 1 • 2 • 3	-3 • -2 • -1 • 0 • 1 • 2 • 3	_____
_____	-3 • -2 • -1 • 0 • 1 • 2 • 3	-3 • -2 • -1 • 0 • 1 • 2 • 3	_____
_____	-3 • -2 • -1 • 0 • 1 • 2 • 3	-3 • -2 • -1 • 0 • 1 • 2 • 3	_____
_____	-3 • -2 • -1 • 0 • 1 • 2 • 3	-3 • -2 • -1 • 0 • 1 • 2 • 3	_____
_____	-3 • -2 • -1 • 0 • 1 • 2 • 3	-3 • -2 • -1 • 0 • 1 • 2 • 3	_____
_____	-3 • -2 • -1 • 0 • 1 • 2 • 3	-3 • -2 • -1 • 0 • 1 • 2 • 3	_____
_____	-3 • -2 • -1 • 0 • 1 • 2 • 3	-3 • -2 • -1 • 0 • 1 • 2 • 3	_____
_____	-3 • -2 • -1 • 0 • 1 • 2 • 3	-3 • -2 • -1 • 0 • 1 • 2 • 3	_____
_____	-3 • -2 • -1 • 0 • 1 • 2 • 3	-3 • -2 • -1 • 0 • 1 • 2 • 3	_____

Appendix D

Financial Support Inventory

This inventory is designed to help clarify the need for financial support. The spouse with this need is to complete the budgets.

Create three budgets in the spaces provided. In the needs budget column, indicate the monthly cost of meeting the necessities of your life, items you would be uncomfortable without. In the income section, include only your spouse's income.

In the wants budget column, indicate the cost of meeting your needs and your wants—reasonable desires that are more costly than necessities. These desires should be as realistic as possible. They should not include a new house, a new car, or luxuries unless you have been wanting these items for some time. Both your income and your spouse's income should appear in this column.

The affordable budget column should include all the needs amounts and only the wants amounts that can be covered by your income and your spouse's income. In other words, your incomes should equal your expenses, and the income minus expenses should be zero. This affordable budget should be used to guide your household finances if both you and your spouse have agreed to the amounts listed.

Payments from the past few months (or year if possible) will help you arrive at correct estimates. Use monthly averages for items that are not paid monthly, such as repairs, vacations, and gifts. Some items, such as your mortgage payment, will be the same amount for both your needs and wants budgets. Other items, such as vacations, will be much more a want than a need. I recommend that you include in your needs budget an emergency fund that is 10 percent of your total budget. In months with no emergency expenses, this money should be saved for the future. Most families suffer needless financial stress when they fail to budget for inevitable emergencies. If you can think of other significant expenses, include these in the blank spaces provided.

If your spouse's income is equal to or greater than the total expenses in the needs budget column, it's sufficient to pay for your needs, and it's meeting your need for financial support. It may actually be covering some of your wants as well. This may not have been obvious, since you have not been dividing your bills into needs and wants. Your need for financial support is still being met when your income is used to pay for wants that are not covered by your spouse's income.

However, if your spouse's income is insufficient to pay for your needs, either you must reduce your household expenses without sacrificing your basic needs or he must increase his income with a pay raise, a new job, or a new career to meet these needs.

Household Expenses and Income	Needs Budget	Wants Budget	Affordable Budget
Expenses			
Taxes			
Income tax	_____	_____	_____
Property tax	_____	_____	_____
Other taxes	_____	_____	_____
Interest			
Mortgage interest	_____	_____	_____
Credit card interest	_____	_____	_____
Automobile loan interest	_____	_____	_____
Other interest	_____	_____	_____

Insurance

Homeowner's insurance	_____	_____	_____
Life insurance	_____	_____	_____
Liability insurance	_____	_____	_____
Auto insurance	_____	_____	_____
Medical and dental insurance	_____	_____	_____
Other insurance	_____	_____	_____

Home Expenses

Home repair	_____	_____	_____
Home remodeling	_____	_____	_____
Home security	_____	_____	_____
Home cleaning	_____	_____	_____
Yard maintenance	_____	_____	_____
Fuel (gas and electricity)	_____	_____	_____
Telephone (landline)	_____	_____	_____
Cell phone purchases	_____	_____	_____
Cell phone plans	_____	_____	_____
Wi-Fi expenses	_____	_____	_____
Garbage removal	_____	_____	_____
Furniture purchases	_____	_____	_____
Appliance purchases	_____	_____	_____
Furniture and appliance repair	_____	_____	_____

Automobiles

Husband's auto depreciation	_____	_____	_____
Husband's auto fuel	_____	_____	_____
Husband's auto maintenance	_____	_____	_____
Wife's auto depreciation	_____	_____	_____
Wife's auto fuel	_____	_____	_____
Wife's auto maintenance	_____	_____	_____
Other auto expenses	_____	_____	_____

Food and Entertainment

Groceries	_____	_____	_____
Dining out	_____	_____	_____
Vacations	_____	_____	_____
Recreational boat expenses	_____	_____	_____
Photography	_____	_____	_____
Magazines and newspapers	_____	_____	_____
Cable TV	_____	_____	_____
Other food and entertainment expenses	_____	_____	_____

Financial Support Inventory

Health

Medical (over insurance)	_____	_____	_____
Dental (over insurance)	_____	_____	_____
Prescription drugs	_____	_____	_____
Nonprescription drugs	_____	_____	_____
Exercise expenses	_____	_____	_____
Special diet expenses	_____	_____	_____
Other health expenses	_____	_____	_____

Clothing

Husband's clothing purchases	_____	_____	_____
Wife's clothing purchases	_____	_____	_____
Children's clothing purchases	_____	_____	_____
Dry cleaning	_____	_____	_____
Alterations and repairs	_____	_____	_____
Other clothing expenses	_____	_____	_____

Personal

Husband's allowance	_____	_____	_____
Wife's allowance	_____	_____	_____
Children's allowances	_____	_____	_____

Gifts

Religious contributions (tithe, religious organizations)	_____	_____	_____
Nonreligious contributions (other charitable causes)	_____	_____	_____
Gifts for special events (birthdays, Christmas, etc.)	_____	_____	_____

Pets

Pet food	_____	_____	_____
Veterinary expenses	_____	_____	_____
Other pet expenses	_____	_____	_____

Savings

Savings for children's education	_____	_____	_____
Savings for retirement (IRAs)	_____	_____	_____
Savings for other projects	_____	_____	_____

Other Household Expenses

Banking	_____	_____	_____
Legal	_____	_____	_____
Accounting and tax preparation	_____	_____	_____
Emergency fund (10%)	_____	_____	_____
Total Household Expenses	_____	_____	_____

Income

Husband's salary	_____	_____	_____
Husband's other income	_____	_____	_____
Wife's salary	_____	_____	_____
Wife's other income	_____	_____	_____
Investment income	_____	_____	_____
Interest income	_____	_____	_____
Total Household Income	_____	_____	_____

Income Minus Expenses   _____   _____   _____

Willard F. Harley, Jr. is a nationally acclaimed clinical psychologist, a marriage counselor, and the bestselling author of numerous books, including *His Needs, Her Needs*; *Love Busters*; *He Wins, She Wins*; *Five Steps to Romantic Love*; *Surviving an Affair*; *Draw Close*; and *His Needs, Her Needs for Parents*. *His Needs, Her Needs: A Six Session Study* is also available as a video curriculum for churches and small groups. His popular website, www.marriagebuilders.com, offers practical solutions to almost any marital problem. He and his wife, Joyce, can be heard weekdays on their internet radio program, *Marriage Builders Radio*.

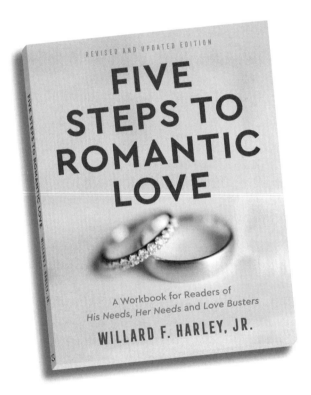

MARRIAGE BUILDERS

Building Marriages To Last A Lifetime

At MarriageBuilders.com, Dr. Harley introduces
you to the best ways to overcome marital conflicts
and the quickest ways to restore love.

Read Dr. Harley's articles, follow the Q&A columns,
interact with other couples on the Forum, and listen to
Dr. Harley and his wife, Joyce, answer your questions on
Marriage Builders® Radio. Learn to become an expert
in making your marriage the best it can be.

*Let Marriage Builders® help you build
a marriage to last a lifetime!*

www.marriagebuilders.com

Interactive 6-Session Study—
Perfect for Small Groups

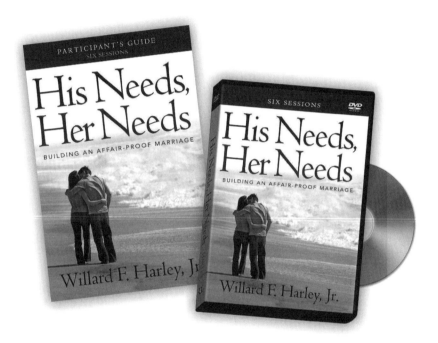

For over twenty-five years, *His Needs, Her Needs* has been transforming marriages all over the world. Now this life-changing book is the basis for an interactive six-week DVD study designed for use in couples' small groups or retreats, in premarital counseling sessions, or by individual couples.

ℛ Revell
a division of Baker Publishing Group
www.RevellBooks.com

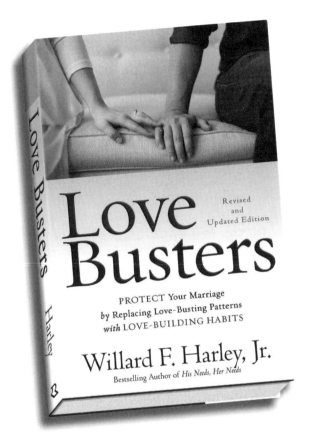